GOD ALONE IS THE TRUTH AND THE WAY

◆

HOW TO SURVIVE THE DECLINE OF AMERICA

Frederick Mahan

T0128160

iUniverse, Inc.
New York Bloomington Shanghai

GOD ALONE IS THE TRUTH AND THE WAY
HOW TO SURVIVE THE DECLINE OF AMERICA

iUniverse books may be ordered through booksellers or by contacting:

iUniverse
1663 Liberty Drive
Bloomington, IN 47403
www.iuniverse.com
1-800-Authors (1-800-288-4677)

Because of the dynamic nature of the Internet, any Web addresses or links contained in this book may have changed since publication and may no longer be valid.

ISBN: 978-0-595-52637-6 (pbk)
ISBN: 978-0-595-62689-2 (ebk)

Printed in the United States of America

I dedicate this book to Dr. Kerry Walters who is an example of one who lives in a state of grace and encourages others to see the good in everything around them.

One of his colleagues shared with him my opinion in an e-mail about the decline of America. Subsequently, I learned he had a similar opinion about the American Dark Age. A short time later, I received several books from a total stranger, an author by the name of Kerry Walters. His writings were similar to Thomas Merton and Henri Nouwen, two of my favorites. I eagerly read the books and found answers to my lifelong questions.

Never before did anyone have the concern for me, a stranger, to send me books that made a big difference in my life. Later, he took time from his busy schedule to patiently listen to many of the problems I address in this book, and he contributed so much to make it a reality.

Kerry is a gifted teacher, writer, actor, Episcopal deacon who "walks the walk." It was no accident that he came into my life, and I want to acknowledge his outstanding contribution to humankind.

Frederick Mahan
San Francisco, CA.

Contents

Part II   Quest for Certainty

Preface

Librarians charged with classifying new books in order to assign them appropriate places on the shelf are going to have a tough time with Frederick Mahan's *God Alone Is The Truth And The Way*. The book, like its author, resists easy compartmentalization.

The book doesn't fit snugly into the genres of philosophy, theology, memoirs, history, or current events, even though there are elements of each of these in it. Nor do its startling conclusions comfortably conform to standard labels such as evangelical, secular, liberal, or conservative. This is because Mr. Mahan is more concerned with following truth where it leads him than in making sure that his opinions are conventionally pleasing.

The upshot is that *God Alone Is The Truth And The Way* is a maverick.

But this is as it should be, because the book's author is something of a maverick himself. Frederick Mahan, the son of an immigrant, is a self-made man. He has achieved the Great American Dream. He is respected in his chosen profession of law. He is wealthy. He is well-read and well-traveled. He has every reason to be proud of his own accomplishments and smugly satisfied with the country in which he has been so successful.

But he is a profoundly dissatisfied man, because he fears that the country in which he lives is slipping into moral and spiritual bankruptcy. He believes that we're entering into a new Dark Age in which, as the poet Yeats wrote, "things fall apart; the centre cannot hold." In this book, which may be accurately described as a sort of "survivor's manual," Mr. Mahan offers us both a diagnosis of how the Great American Dream has turned into the Great American Nightmare, and some suggestions on how to get through the coming chaos. His suggestions are based in part on his deep-seated faith—deep-seated, mind you, *not* simplistic—in part on his rich life experience, and in part on his astoundingly wide reading. The convergence of these three strands is what makes the book difficult to classify. It's also what makes it provocative and challenging.

Mr. Mahan offers no quick fixes or magical solutions in *God Alone Is The Truth And The Way*. Indeed, he doubts that any are to be found (in fact, the demand for quick fixes is part of our problem). But he does a remarkable job of outlining the symptoms of our present dis-ease as well as the remedies available to us. *God Alone Is The Truth And The Way* is not an especially pleasant book to read, because it refuses to sugarcoat the pill. But it *is* an essential book.

Kerry Walters
William Bittinger Professor of Philosophy
Gettysburg College
Gettysburg, Pennsylvania

Introduction

The San Francisco dockworker Eric Hoffer became a noted philosopher, a best-selling author, and an acute observer of American life. In my own way, over the past fifty years, I have observed the out-of-control decadence and intemperance in America.

I am a retired trial attorney of forty-four years, an active businessman, a past board member of two nonprofit corporations and a past president of one, a symphony and opera patron, a big-time supporter of higher education, a past member of my church's council, and a benefactor of numerous charities that care for those who need assistance. I have read countless books, attended an untold number of lectures, and maintained a complete library on the subjects addressed in this book. I keep company with some of the wisest people in America. More importantly, I am an informed citizen who voted for fifty-four years, with few exceptions. My companions and I know what is going on economically, politically, morally, spiritually, and academically in America.

Socrates was an unpublished author without credentials. Plato chronicled the ideas of Socrates and most likely left it to posterity to make its conclusions. In some instances, I cannot document my opinions and conclusions based on experience and observations. I am writing about political theology, not the hard sciences. Nonetheless, I encourage my readers to test all of my statements.

After World War II, affluence led to higher education, greater leisure, and more opportunities for service to others; however, negative trends occurred, including substance abuse, juvenile delinquency, crime, and divorce. Those who did not exercise moderation in the accumulation of wealth and power became slaves to greed, avarice, gluttony, and lust.

Within the past fifty years, I have witnessed radical changes in the behavior and attitudes of many citizens that have accelerated the decline of the American culture. Spin doctors have replaced the educators of virtue, truth, and service. Ancient wisdom has been replaced with an identity crisis—narcissism gone haywire. I need only mention the pop-star singers who send teenaged children into frenzies with their sexually explicit gyrations. Mob mentality has replaced responsible behavior by teenagers and college students.

In my considered opinion, the irresponsible behavior of American presidents, corporate officers, and politicians; the combative attitude of the unemployed and "rebels with a cause" (advocates of same-sex marriage and abortion); and the reckless conduct of the government have caused the irreversible decline of America. Dissatisfied and desperate seniors, military families, and middle- to lower-class families are barely able to survive. Nevertheless, there are options. With faith in almighty God, the author of truth, we can live in this declining nation with a sense of direction and peace of mind.

In the final analysis, what we do in response to this tragedy is a matter of choice. People must sacrifice for their freedom; otherwise, that freedom will vanish.

I have found history to be a more reliable source of information about human nature than philosophy or psychology. Philosophers wonder about absolute reality, creation, nature, love, and the human condition. They debate with one another about the merits of their respective theories. But philosophies fade away. Psychiatrists closely observe the passions, desires, and behavior of individuals. Historians, on the other hand, chronicle the behavior, ideas, religions, philosophies, and emotions of mankind. Some have recorded similar causes for the rise and fall of every civilization. After the fall of a nation, they report a standstill in the pursuit of learning and advancement of understanding. This standstill is a dark age. Following the dark age, there is usually a renaissance or rebirth.

Part I: The Dark Age

In the first section of this book, I will describe the behavior, mentality, attitudes, beliefs, and lies of those who I believe have accelerated the decline of American culture. I will analyze the factors that caused the decline of other Western civilizations. I will share with readers what others have said in support of their conclusions about the decline of other civilizations. I will expand on these subjects with insights from history, religion, literature, and philosophy.

Part II: Quest for Certainty

In the second section of this book, I will share with readers what I have learned from the writings of gifted individuals who know about love, marriage, democracy, truth, and purpose. Although I have no suggestions for changing American culture, I will recommend ways to live through these dark days.

Part III: Resurrection

In the third section, I will tell readers about my disappointments, failures, sufferings, feelings, and discoveries. This is not an autobiography; I simply hope to encourage others with an account of my spiritual failures and successes. I also invite readers to explore a relationship with God as embodied in Jesus Christ. My message is not a "call to the altar"; it is a wake-up call by an amateur historian and philosopher who believes in one god who created heaven and earth. Many people think I am a court jester, but I thank God that I am like other men: a sinner saved by grace.

In my growing-up years, I experienced and witnessed a lot of injustice. I could not reconcile it with what I heard and read about the principles set forth in the U. S. Constitution. My secondary-school teachers taught me that I was equal to other citizens by law, and that there was liberty and justice for all. They taught me that the president of the United States places his hand on the Bible and takes an oath that he will preserve, protect, and defend the Constitution of the United States. They taught me that he is elected by an honest vote count. They told me that the state and federal governments were responsible for providing me with a good education and that all students, regardless of their race or color, would be treated equally.

However, I witnessed firsthand the prejudice against immigrants. Because of my desire to understand and correct the prejudice, I decided to become a lawyer. It was in law school that I acquired the ability and the habit of analyzing everything to determine its truth. Having acquired this skill, I analyzed my beliefs, their sources, and their trustworthiness.

In the chapters that follow, I will describe in detail what I discovered about the validity of the information I received and relied on for most of my life.

In this book, I swear to tell the truth, with reasonable certainty. Some of the statements presented here are a synthesis of my views and those of others. I leave it to you, the reader, to disbelieve all of the views expressed until you have tested their credibility with your own heart and mind.

PART I
The Dark Age

1

The Decline and Fall of American Culture

THE AMERICAN DREAM

The American dream was the chief reason for my parents' desire to come to America. They saw in this country an opportunity to freely live and worship. As my parents did, I embraced this dream and believed that with talent, intelligence, and a willingness to work extremely hard, I would have an unwavering and righteous life.

"American dream" is a phrase created by James Truslow Adams in his 1931 book *The Epic of America*.[1] The phrase refers to an approach to government and economics different from the traditional models. For me, the phrase means "success in life because of hard work."

Too many Americans seem to have an unrealistic dream of an idyllic utopia—a hidden paradise to be available when they win the lottery, when their start-up company goes public, or when their elected representatives materialize the utopia. I also believe many people now use the phrase "American way" to mean "the end justifies the means." In other words, do whatever it takes to get everything for nothing. Put it on the expense account. There is no down payment. Get government grants for anything your heart desires.

From 1931, the year of my birth, until 1952, the year I graduated from college, most Americans could not afford instant gratification and did not have the time or the money to spend on hedonistic lifestyles. In the early fifties, the "American way" took on an expanded meaning that became full blown in the sixties with consumerism: purchasing goods or consuming materials in excess of basic needs.

---

1.   James Truslow Adams, *The Epic of America*, (New York: Simon Publications, 2001).

CAUSES OF THE FALL OF ROME

Edward Gibbon, in his classic 1776 book *The Decline and Fall of the Roman Empire*,[2] gives some basic reasons for the fall of Rome: "the undermining of the sanctity of the home; a rapid increase in divorce; the development of huge armaments and the neglect of the enemy within; moral degeneracy (sexual perversion, such as homosexuality); and the deterioration of religious vitality, with formalism supplanting faith and impotence replacing power." Mr. Gibbons noted that before the first century BC, Rome's affluence corrupted its political system. Political zealots bribed voters and created an impasse in the senate. Consequently, there was injustice, lawlessness, and misuse of public funds.

I have observed how affluence has corrupted our political system as well. Partisan politics in Congress in the past two years (and on many other occasions) have brought the affairs of government to a standstill. Government officials resigned to avoid impeachment; numerous elected representatives received felony convictions. Both parties use loopholes in the law governing campaign contributions in order to swing the votes in their favor.

Just as ancient Rome developed huge armaments and neglected its enemy within, the United States uses its military force to build its empire, yet it neglects homeland security by failing to stop terrorists and illegal aliens from invading the country.

Moral degeneracy and the deterioration of religious fervor have also eroded the American dream and contributed to the decline of American culture. Moral degenerates, in conflict with the Ten Commandments, clamor to remove them from the Supreme Court building and to remove God from our coinage. The Supreme Court might consider a compromise: "In God we do not trust." These words more closely match the reality.

I offer the following surveys, and you decide whether or not religious vitality, too, has rapidly deteriorated.

> In August 2006, an article reported that the Evangelical Lutheran Church in America had fewer baptized members since 2004. The ELCA report was said to reflect that of many other churches based in the United States. The report also revealed a steep drop in membership of United Methodist churches in 2005.[3]

---

2.   Edward Gibbon, Decline and Fall of the Roman Empire, (1776) Christian Classics Etherial Library, http://www.ccel.org/ccel/gibbon/decline/files/decline.html (accessed January 31, 2007).

A recent study by Fordham University professor James Lothian concluded that 65 percent of Catholics went to Sunday Mass in 1965. Lothian found that the rate had dropped to 25 percent in 2000. Five hundred and forty-nine parishes were without a resident priest in 1965. In 2002, 2,928 parishes were without priests.[4]

CORRUPT REPRESENTATIVES AND GOVERNMENT SPENDING

Deficit spending, outrageous taxes, and a wasteful bureaucratic government are threatening the integrity and survival of American culture. Bureaucracy is like an amoeba; when divided, the portion containing the nucleus forms a new bureaucracy and continues spending revenue, while the other portion lives as long as its revenue lasts. Legislators squabble about which party is misusing public funds, but no one is blameless.

Tax revenue is the most apparent source of funds for federal spending, and the Congress enacts tax laws to effect social and economic change. I believe that federal and state legislators do not answer to anyone for their reckless spending or for enacting laws that benefit a few to the detriment of others.

J. T. Wilson Field in Somerset, Kentucky, got more than $12 million since 2001, much of it through the influence of Rep. Hal Rogers, a longtime Republican member of the House Appropriations Committee who uses the airfield for trips home. Wilson Field is home base to twenty-six small planes and one jet. Despite millions in improvements, including a passenger terminal, the airport has yet to see scheduled commercial service.[5]

Lobbyists have gained larger roles in the Democratic Congress, notwithstanding the fact that Nancy Pelosi was highly critical of the Republicans for bowing to pressure from lobbyists during the years when they were in the majority in Congress. Now that the Democrats are the majority party, they receive many favors

---

3.   Lillian Kwon, *Christian Post Reporter*, (Aug. 02 2006). http://www.christianpost.com/article/20060802/23434

4.   Ibid. Statistics from "Index of Leading Catholic Indicators," by Kenneth Jones *(Lowell, MI: These Last Days Ministries, Inc. 2005) http://www.tldm.org*. Statistics are originally from Kenneth Jones' Index of Leading Catholic Indicators.
      Copyright © These Last Days Ministries, Inc. 1996–2005. All rights reserved. P.O. Box 40 Lowell, MI 49331-0040 http://www.tldm.org

5.   www.travelindustrydeals.com/news/

from lobbyists in exchange for legislation that benefits clients of lobbyists. Members of Congress live the high life from the money and gifts they receive in exchange for favors they give to their benefactors. Taxpayers, and those in need of social welfare, end up the losers.

The national debt, taxes to pay the interest, and inflation will be a burden for future generations. The American dream may well be a nightmare for many.

CORPORATE ABUSE

Corporations ruthlessly abuse consumers with dangerous products and false advertisements that appeal to unsuspecting buyers. Corporations encourage excessive spending, offer easy credit, and lure low-income buyers to purchase merchandise they cannot afford.

Corporations use their ill-gotten gains to implement social policy and control universities' research programs with conditional grants. In addition, corporations pollute the environment, deny employees adequate wages and benefits, and outsource jobs to countries that provide cheap labor. They do all this with the sanction of federal and state governments. The United States Supreme Court and several state governments allow corporate banks to charge unconscionable interest rates on credit card balances so consumers can enrich the banking institutions that lobby the elected representatives.

EDUCATION

Many universities and colleges are in the business of making a profit, and they are lowering the standards of education in order to satisfy the wishes of the student body—thereby increasing applications, enrollment, and the student retention rate. For example, contemporary civilization, authors of the Western literary tradition, foreign languages, music appreciation, and Judeo-Christian subjects were required courses at the liberal arts college I attended. Some of these courses have been eliminated or are no longer prerequisites for graduation, because many students did not want to take them.

The present chancellor at the University of California, San Francisco School of Medicine and several other illustrious alumni of the college conducted a well-attended seminar at my fiftieth reunion. They emphasized the importance of the abovementioned courses in helping graduates add unselfish service to their careers. The chancellor (who won a Nobel Prize for his research in cancer) said that many college graduates have the ability to do medical research, but few experience the happiness gained from doing research to find a cure for a life-threatening disease. In conclusion, there is a vast difference between using higher education for the sole purpose of earning a higher income and using it for the additional purpose of reducing human misery.

Google the phrase "dumbing down," and you will find that books originally for the middle grades have been certified as being appropriate for high school students; textbooks for high schools have appeared as college textbooks. Generally speaking, for decades, there has been a dishonorable inflation of grades. Professors in an untold number of colleges are criticized if they do not give a student a *B*, and many *B* students who have an exaggerated opinion of their performance now demand *A* grades.

This grade inflation has replaced an honest evaluation of students' comprehension. Some graduates of our prestigious educational institutions use the inflated grades in their résumés and obtain high-paying jobs in the corporate asylum. Meanwhile, their alma maters solicit grants from corporate employers that are in the business of manipulating research from the universities.

I obtained much of my information about the condition of the educational system in America from newspapers, magazines, and books on the subject. If you are in doubt, check it out. Here are only a few examples:

"Too many teacher colleges major in mediocrity" (*USA Today*, March 17, 2002, http://www.usatoday.com/news/opinion/2002/03/18/nceditf.htm)

"Education and the Dangers of Parental Complacency," by Kate O'Beirne (http://www.pisd.org/voices/complacent)

James Michener, *This Noble Land: My Vision for America* (New York: Ballantine Books, 1997)

Charles J. Sykes, *Dumbing Down Our Kids: Why American Children Feel Good About Themselves But Can't Read, Write, or Add* (St. Martin's Griffin: New York, 1995.)

ENTERTAINMENT

Once upon a time, Hollywood had its own moral code. Nowadays, because of the media, families are exposed to more violence than in prior generations. The average viewer can see levels of violence exceeding those of the Roman gladiator games. Many of the movies seen at home would not even have been shown in theaters forty years ago.

The Bible teaches that "as a man thinks in his heart, so is he" (Prov. 23:7). What we view and what we think about affects our actions.

PEACE IN THE MIDDLE EAST

Another reason Rome collapsed was its failure to solve the problems in the Middle East. Self-defeating Roman victories in Iran were short-lived and part of a conflict that lasted for more than six centuries.

The George W. Bush administration believed that it could succeed in establishing capitalist democracies in the Middle East. The current and past presidents, members of Congress, and people in the State Department have been ignorant and arrogant about foreign affairs.

Arabic was my native tongue, and I spoke it fluently for four decades. In the military, I was a liaison between Saudi Arabian officers and their American flight instructors. I befriended Iranian and Iraqi students studying comparative law in the United States. I have adult friends and acquaintances that were reared in the Middle East. I can honestly say that one needs to speak the language of a country in order to know the heart and soul of the natives. I observe how Arabic-speaking people light up when I speak Arabic to them. They greet me with the word *ahlain* ("double welcome"), and we respect one another as family.

To understand the troubles that beset the Middle East, one must comprehend the mentality and ideology of the people. The average Muslim does not want the elusive freedom of Western civilization. He has always feared another crusade and fears even more that capitalism and a democracy will do in the Muslim world what they have done in the United States. Since he has never experienced the American mentality and democracy firsthand, he is not eager to embrace it.

NATIONAL DEBT

According to the Honorable David M. Walker, comptroller general of the United States, the federal budget deficit in 2004 was close to $567 billion. The comptroller general stated that the long-term liabilities and commitments in 2004 were over $43 trillion and that our country has the lowest overall savings rate of any major industrial nation. Also, the average family has a credit-card balance of thousands of dollars. In 2005, personal bankruptcies reached an all-time record. The trade deficit reached a record of $618 billion in 2004. China and Japan have been funding our trade deficit.[6]

Every day, we read about a natural disaster that requires billions in federal aid. Neither the USGS nor CalTech scientists have ever predicted a major earthquake, nor do they know how or expect to know how anytime in the foreseeable future; however, based on scientific data, scientists estimate that over the next thirty years, the probability of a major earthquake occurring in the San Francisco Bay Area is 67 percent, and it is 60 percent in Southern California.[7]

From Maine to Texas, our coastline is filled with new homes, condominium towers, and cities built on sand, waiting for the next storm to threaten its residents and their dreams. A large portion of the coastal areas, with high population densities, is subject to inundation from a hurricane's storm surge, which historically has caused the greatest loss of life and extreme property damage.

In the United States, tornadoes are found most frequently east of the Rocky Mountains during the spring and summer months. The National Severe Storms Laboratory provides information about tornadoes on their Web site. Wind speeds in the most violent tornadoes can be as high as 300 miles per hour. Wind speeds that high can cause automobiles to become airborne, rip ordinary homes to shreds, and turn broken glass and other debris into lethal missiles. The biggest threat to living creatures (including humans) from tornadoes is from flying debris and from being tossed about in the wind.[8]

Residents of the California coast are vulnerable to tsunamis caused by distant events such as an earthquake in Alaska or Japan, or by local earthquakes. Of par-

---

6.   David M. Walker, "The Leadership Gap and America's Fiscal Future," U.S. Government Accountability Office Address Given Before The Conference Board, New York, New York, October 6, 2005, as quoted in http://www.gao.gov/cghome/conferenceboardspeech1062005.pdf (accessed January 31, 2007).

7.   www.depts.ttu.edu/MuseumTTU/disasters/

8.   ibid

ticular concern would be an earthquake along the Juan de Fuca Subduction Zone, which runs along the coast from Northern California into Canada[9].

Providing emergency relief after any of these disasters would put the United States deeper into debt. The statistics scare the hell out of me and, as a child born in the Depression, I cannot ignore the already alarming national debt. My only solace is to walk through the house, urging my family to turn off the lights and eat all of the food on their plates.

FINANCIAL AID TO IMMIGRANTS

The immigrants of the late nineteenth and early twentieth centuries did not receive entitlements. They relied on industriousness to produce the lifestyles they earned. They had pride in being self-reliant. Families who prospered assisted others. Work was the only option, and it was a joy to experience the results of their labor.

George J. Borjas is the Robert W. Scrivner Professor of Economics and Social Policy. He received his PhD in economics from Columbia. His teaching and research interests focus on the impact of government regulations on labor markets, with an emphasis on the economic impact of immigration. According to Dr. Borjas and economist Lynette Hilton, from 1996 forward, immigrant (noncitizen) households received 21 percent of various types of assistance, as compared with only 14 percent of native households. Earlier immigrants influence the types of benefits received by recently arrived immigrants. Ethnic networks pass on information to new immigrants about the availability of particular benefits. Many recently arrived immigrants and illegal immigrants do not subscribe to the principle that there is no such thing as a free lunch.[10]

This assistance is alarming because our government continues in the tradition of substituting entitlements for self-reliance. It allows poor immigrants, legal and illegal, into the country without an employment program. The immigration quota should be less than the number of jobs available. Surely, U.S. Citizenship and Immigration Services inquire about the skills of each immigrant and compare them with American needs. If there is no prospect for employment because

---

9.   www.dominican.edu/…/new-study-examines-tsunami-awareness-preparedness-in-northern-california/

10. George J. Borjas and Lynette Hilton, "Immigration and the Welfare State: Immigrant Participation in Means-Tested Entitlement Programs," *Quarterly Journal of Economics*, v. III, no. 2 (May 1996), pp. 575–604.

of age, language deficiency, or physical or mental problems, then U.S. taxpayers will bear the burden of an immigrant's unemployment, medical, and education benefits.

DIMINISHING EMPLOYMENT OPPORTUNITIES

Farmers in many states hire illegal immigrants to pick crops. Because of the long hours and low wages farmers offer, few Americans are willing to work in the fields that produce the food we eat. Consequently, many Americans work elsewhere for fewer hours and the same low wages paid to illegal immigrants. If they cannot find employment elsewhere, they may be entitled to state and federal government unemployment benefits. This example is a symptom of a more serious disease: management and labor irresponsibility.

Managers are interested more in the bottom line than in the welfare of their employees. Rather than pay competitive wages and incur the expense of major medical and retirement benefits, management often outsources labor overseas. One apparent solution to outsourcing is to keep a grip on inflation, so that management can provide reasonable wages and benefits to employees. In the same way, laborers should not demand "two chickens in every pot and two cars in every garage." What was once a luxury is now deemed a necessity; the American dream is an expensive illusion created by greed and envy. Perhaps it is time for workers to reduce their consumption of unnecessary and expensive entertainment and recreational items. Management and labor must exercise financial responsibility and put an end to excesses.

MILITARY EMPIRE

Our effort to build a military empire is transforming America. We spend revenue on weaponry and to maintain troops in many other countries. In addition, we do not hesitate to intervene in the affairs of other countries, on the claim that it is in the interest of homeland security. Taxpayers pick up the cost for protecting the interests of private American enterprises overseas. Tax revenue is being diverted from funds reserved for future obligations. In some instances, the budgets of agencies that render various public services are cut in order to balance the budget or reduce the deficit. It matters not what source is used to build a military empire; the taxpayers are picking up the tab.

The State Department and executive branch, since the time of President McKinley, have planned to expand U.S. economic interest in other countries. President Jefferson initiated the program with the purchase of the Louisiana Territory.

The United States supports corrupt governments that favor its economic interests at the time. We supported the shah of Iran, even though thousands of Iranians were dying of malnutrition. After the shah's departure, the United States supported Saddam Hussein in the war against Iran. We supported Osama bin Laden in the Afghan war against Russia. We took sides in Somalia, Bosnia, and Croatia. It's funny how so many of our "allies" seem to turn against us, using the weapons we provide them.

The first Gulf War is another example of military imperialism. It is all about oil. The American taxpayers are paying the price, and I am referring to the loss of American men and women, not to the price at the pump.

In his online article entitled "With Few Actively Engaged, U.S. Is a Nation of Bystanders in War on Terrorism," David Wood maintains that the majority of Americans are detached and indifferent to the global war on terrorism. In the 1980s, more than half of high school males would volunteer for a "necessary" war. At present, two-thirds of the young men surveyed by the Department of Defense said they would not volunteer for military duty, even in a crisis.[11]

I will not argue against the facts. The United States is a nation of bystanders in the war on terrorism, and justly so. I, for one, am no longer willing to support military imperialism so that corrupt politicians and corporate officers can make preemptive war for personal gain. It is time to stop appealing to young people's sense of duty to die for their country and freedom. The war in Iraq is not a war on terrorism, and our potential allies know it.

Circumstances today are different from those in World War II and World War I. Imperialist governments attacked us, and we fought against oppression. The same was true in the war for independence.

The United States invaded Iraq to make certain that it did not have weapons of mass destruction. As it turned out, Iraq did not have such weapons, and the United States must contend with a civil war with doubtful results and the needless loss of young Americans. President Bush refuses to take responsibility for his decision to shoot first and ask questions later.

---

11. David Wood, "With Few Actively Engaged, U.S. Is Nation of Bystanders in War on Terrorism," Newhouse News Service, 2004, http://www.newhousenews.com/archive/wood072004.html.

EPIDEMIC PERSONAL DEBT

In 1978, the Supreme Court changed the interpretation of usury laws with a ruling in the case of *Marquette National Bank of Minneapolis v. First Omaha Service Corp.*[12] *Usury* is the lending of money at an unreasonably high interest rate, and this rate is defined at the state level. The Supreme Court determined that the usury issue was a legislative problem for Congress. The court held that Section 85 of the National Bank Act allowed a lender to charge the highest interest rate allowed in the lender's home state, regardless of whether a lower rate existed in the customer's state of residence.

After this decision, South Dakota, Delaware, and other states seized the opportunity to deregulate interest, in order to attract banks and other consumer lenders. In 1981, Citicorp established a new national bank and credit-card processing center in Sioux Falls, South Dakota. These states allowed Citicorp to charge credit-card holders an unlimited amount of interest.

There has been an astronomical increase in credit-card debt because the credit industry has made borrowing easy. In 1968, consumers' total credit debt was $8 billion (in current dollars). Now, according to a Federal Reserve Bank report from June 2007, the total exceeds $880 billion.

Every year, I receive numerous preapproved credit-card offers. An astounding number of Americans find themselves in serious financial trouble due to layoffs, company downsizing, merging corporations, and fluctuation in the stock market. Families get into debt trying to pay the principal and the exorbitant interest on their credit cards. Because of inflation, middle-class families have little discretionary income. When credit-card payments become unmanageable, a family may take on a second mortgage to consolidate all that debt. A significant number of Americans file for bankruptcy due to unemployment, medical problems, or family breakups that result in a staggering increase in credit-card debt. But sadly, no law exists that prevents financial institutions from offering credit to individuals who cannot realistically pay back their existing debt, let alone any more they may incur with additional credit.

There is life after debt, but there is no easy out. Here is my method for achieving financial security; it may be of help to anyone in a financial crisis:

---

12. Marquette National Bank of Minneapolis v. First Omaha Service Corp, 439 U.S. 299 (1978).

- Pay the monthly balance within the allotted time. I have no occasion to transfer high-interest credit-card debt to a lower-interest card.

- Have a budget, and never spend in excess of your income. I prioritize my spending and save for a rainy day.

- Pay off your credit-card debt with savings. If there is no balance on the card, the credit limit will be available for emergency needs.

- Pay off consumer debt with a home-equity loan. Lower interest rates and tax deductibility are two advantages.

- On purchases made with a debit card, the money comes directly out of the checking account.

- Limit credit-card purchases to the day-to-day necessities you are obliged to purchase regularly—gas and groceries, for instance—and that you'd normally pay for with cash.

The bankruptcy laws have changed, limiting the discharge of certain debts. If your debts are 50 percent or more of your annual income, then seriously consider filing bankruptcy.

OUR RESPONSIBILITY

Do you have any responsibility to fulfill, revise, or rescue the American dream? If you do, how would you do it? Why would you do it? For whom would you do it? If you did it before, would you do it again? Since it is a lifelong effort, would you consult with anyone before you accepted the responsibility?

Before you answer, recall the myth of Sisyphus, a character destined to roll a boulder up a mountain for one thousand years. In my opinion, the task of rescuing the American dream will be as arduous. Would you reconsider the decisions you made that might have led you to fulfill the dream? What would you do to revise or rescue the dream?

The dream lured me, because I wanted to be somebody. I was not willing to live an ordinary, boring life. The dream offered challenge and adventure. It did not occur to me that the fulfillment of a dream could be like dust in the wind and the acquisition of stuff without meaning.

The fulfillment of a dream reminds me of the rich young ruler in Jesus' parable. When Jesus asked him to sell all his stuff and give it to the poor, the ruler went away, weeping. In past times, I too wept. Now I recommend to others that they revise their dream.

The dream is a conundrum. Without the dream, great things cannot be done. On the other hand, the dream can become a nightmare if it is not revised. Much depends on revising our dreams as we mature. My dream changed from the desire to be somebody to the desire to help somebody.

God made me somebody by transforming me into a more selfless nobody. Along the way, I began to carry less baggage. I retained the original meaning of the American dream: success through hard work.

God gives us success so that we can do his will. At times, we will not have the power to accomplish our plans, because they are not in accordance with his will; nevertheless, in success or failure, God is always with us.

Isaac asked his son, "How did you find it so quickly, my son?"
"The Lord your God gave me success," he replied.

Genesis 39:3

In everything he did he had great success, because the Lord was with him.

1 Samuel 18:14

Do I have any power to help myself, now that success has been driven from me?

Job 6:13

"Therefore I tell you, do not be anxious about your life, what you shall eat or what you shall drink, nor about your body, what you shall put on. Is not life more than food, and the body more than clothing?"

Matthew 6:25

2

Accountability

There is no freedom without responsibility. In my opinion, people will not be responsible if they are not held to answer for their misdeeds. It is obvious to me that undisciplined and untrustworthy family members, corporate officers, elected representatives, educators, etc. were not held to answer for their misdeeds in their formative years.

When I was eight years old, my third-grade teacher told me about George Washington cutting down the cherry tree and acknowledging his misdeed. Around the same time, I heard about how honest Abe Lincoln walked several miles to return a small sum of money he owed to an individual. These stories had a positive effect on me; however, some irresponsible citizens want to rewrite American history books to conform to the character traits of recent presidents and call these two stories deceitful. Others go so far as to claim that some of Honest Abe's letters to male friends establish that he was a homosexual.[1]

From the story of Washington, children learn that they are not to tell lies in order to cover up wrongdoings. I do not excuse white lies, and I refrain from telling them. Nowadays, self-righteous hypocrites refuse to tell their children myths for fear that they will think that their parents are deceiving them. I venture to say that such parents cause their children greater harm, because many myths teach children to be trustworthy and responsible.

Perhaps Richard M. Nixon, William Jefferson Clinton, and George W. Bush did not believe the cherry tree story, that Lincoln was honest, and that there are truths in myths. What I find difficult to believe is that Clinton, the Rhodes Scholar, would tarnish the office of president of the United States. He had the nerve to walk across the White House lawn with his family, carrying a Bible.

Elsewhere in this book, I state at length several tragic flaws in the character development of many Americans. In this chapter, I will specifically emphasize the

---

1.   Jennifer Viegas, "Book Questions Abraham Lincoln's Sexuality" Discovery.com, Dec. 8, 2004, accessed 2/11/07.

leniency of parents and teachers in rearing children. In addition, during the last half of the twentieth century, Americans have failed to demand legal and moral responsibility from members of their families, educators, elected representatives, the media, the clergy, and business people.

There has been a state of lawlessness or political disorder due to the leniency of parents, the judicial system, school administrations, and religious institutions. It is anybody's guess why it started; however, I venture to say that the federal government was largely responsible for the lawlessness. The United States has fought numerous needless wars within the past fifty years. I need mention only the Vietnam War and its aftermath. That war ushered in the hippie drug generation and the sexual revolution. During World War II, Americans complained bitterly about the atrocities committed by Germans and Japanese on American servicemen. We professed to have a higher regard for human life. The American atrocities in Vietnam seemed unusual because they were as unconscionable as those committed by the Germans and Japanese. Since that time, there have been incidents of inhumane torture of prisoners at Abu Ghraib.

It is doubtful that there are statistics on the increase of torture and other atrocities by American servicemen. Nevertheless, I believe that morality has changed for the worse in America. I, for one, think that Americans do not see the danger that the United States will fall because of the enemy within.

For some unknown reason, parents seemed unable to discipline children who were influenced by the antiwar movement and the rebellion against moral standards. In addition, numerous parents cast off family values and indulged in sexual promiscuity and substance abuse.

In my opinion, the Vietnam War took its toll on American values. That does not mean that America was a nation of God-fearing people; however, it gave them an excuse to start living devil-may-care lives.

Individuals have little, if any, say about a commander-in-chief's decision in favor of a preemptive war. Their only remedy is to vote the bums out of office. The tragedy is that those who take their place are also a bunch of bums.

As far as I am concerned, there is no alternative to accountability and legal and moral responsibility. In addition, no one is beyond the rule of legal and moral law. If one is beyond the rules, then all are beyond them, and the result is anarchy. All family members must be accountable to one another, clergymen must be accountable to their congregations, and school administrators must be accountable to parents.

When we are accountable, we avoid self-destruction. Anyone convicted of a crime should suffer the consequences, whether he or she is the president of the

United States, an army general, a citizen, or a family member. Presidential pardons should be repealed, and so should parole in cases of capital punishment.

Most Americans are obsessed with freedom for themselves; therefore, they have no reason to deny freedom to others. But freedom without responsibility is a utopian society having no government, composed of individuals who enjoy complete freedom. If this happens, then anything goes. Perhaps the best examples of such societies are Sodom and Gomorrah and Jericho.

What is wrong with our government besides all that I have mentioned so far? How did the representatives get there, and how do we get rid of them? Assuming that we can get rid of them, how can we exclude accountability-challenged people from office? If this cannot be accomplished, then what can we do as individuals? I will take a few moments to reason about the answers.

You and I elected them. We depended on their campaign promises. We were naïve to believe that no child would be left behind. We read his lips and believed that there would not be new taxes. We believed that Hillary Clinton would draft a health insurance program that Congress would pass into law. Republican and Democratic senators and congresspersons praised Hillary for her outstanding talents. As did George W. Bush, she will hoodwink the voters into believing that she is a political savior. The voters never seem to learn that there are no individuals on the political horizon who are gifted enough to be political saviors, controlling a partisan Congress. Between two evils, chose neither.

Several universities have schools of government. I will only mention Harvard University's JFK School of Government. David R. Gergen is professor of public leadership and the director of the Center for Public Leadership. Over the past three decades, he has served as an advisor to four presidents: Richard Nixon, Gerald Ford, Ronald Reagan, and William J. Clinton. You may have seen him on CNN. He speaks bluntly about the mistakes made by George W. in Iraq.

When the facts so warrant, it would be gross negligence if an internist failed to call in a specialist for a second opinion. The same duty should apply to all branches of government. Four presidents conferred with Mr. Gergen over a period of thirty years. Mr. Bush was responsible enough to retain the services of Ambassador L. Paul Bremer to act as presidential envoy. The president has the unique opportunity to retain the best minds in the world to advise him on any given subject. Other than those who publicly stated their involvement with Mr. Bush's decision to invade Iraq, no other advisers were mentioned.

Mr. Bush stubbornly resisted all advice to dismiss Secretary Rumsfeld. Ambassador Bremer revealed the possible failure of the administration and the Pentagon in Iraq. Even members of his party have publicly stated that there were mistakes made in Iraq. Mr. Bush's foolish mistakes cost the lives of several thousand servicemen and caused their families to suffer.

Prior to his second term, there was a strong link between the availability of expert advisors, the failure of the president to use them, and the need for his accountability. Those who were responsible for his second term have already been held accountable, in that they will suffer the consequences of a lame duck president.

Insofar as Mr. Bush is concerned, I, for one, will hold his party accountable for shrewd campaigning and pulling the wool over the eyes of the conservative right in order to return Mr. Bush to the White House.

Hopefully, historians will mention Cindy Sheehan as a patriot. After she lost her son in Iraq, she demonstrated against the war, but to no avail. She left the Democratic Party because Hillary Clinton would not take a stand against the war. Mrs. Clinton did not want to alienate those who support the war. The voters are responsible for rescuing the American way; however, from the look of things, there is no candidate in either party who has the qualifications to rescue America.

Jay Garner, a retired Army general turned defense contractor, was the first U.S. administrator of post-invasion Iraq. He appointed Kimberly Olson, a highly decorated air force colonel, to serve as his chief assistant to head up the U.S. occupation of Iraq in 2003.

The *Los Angeles Times* reported on April 19, 2006 that Ms. Olson appeared before a military tribunal on charges of using her position as Jay Garner's executive officer to win more than $3 million in contracts for a private security firm with which she was associated.[2]

Garner was relieved in May 2003, and Paul Bremer became the presidential envoy to Iraq on May 6, 2003; in this capacity, he was the administrator of the Coalition Provisional Authority.[3] He received his BA from Yale University, a CEP from the Institut D'Etudes Politiques of the University of Paris, and an MBA from Harvard.

In an exclusive interview with NBC's Brian Williams, Paul Bremer revealed the possible failures by top officials at the White House and the Pentagon. Bremer candidly told Williams, "I believe I did everything I could do. My view is in government, you have an obligation to tell the president what you think. You

---

2.   Jeff Lincoln, More revelations of US profiteering and corruption in Iraq, April 21 2006, Published by the Committee of the International Fourth International (ICFI) wsws.org (accessed 2/9/2007)

3.   Ibid.

should do that in private through appropriate channels, as I tried to do. The president, in the end, is responsible for making decisions."[4]

INCOMPETENCE WITHOUT ACCOUNTABILITY

As Americans, we reasonably expect that at the higher levels of government, there are competent individuals who take action to avoid national catastrophes; however, it is not so. We witnessed unbelievable incompetence in the World Trade Center and Hurricane Katrina tragedies.

When I was in the military, I reported to my squadron commander that three cadets were violating flight regulations and endangering their lives and those of others. The commander refused to take action against them, because the air force needed pilots and their training had cost the government a substantial sum. Subsequently, one of the three attempted to fly under a bridge and crashed into the side of it. The other two were in gunnery training, and against regulations, they were dog fighting. They and one outstanding pilot died in a midair collision.

In World War II, the highest military command had knowledge that the Japanese intended to bomb Pearl Harbor. A critical alert message did not reach the responsible commander quickly enough, and the military was unprepared when the attack occurred. Thousands died because a few noncommissioned and general-grade officers behaved irresponsibly; however, they were never held accountable.

The moral of this story is that our leaders in high places are incompetent to a large degree. Even worse, the president and other elected representatives are not accountable to anyone. Long after the disasters, the media revealed their incompetence and lack of accountability.

After the Watergate scandal, state bar associations disbarred many lawyers, who subsequently served time in prison; however, President Ford pardoned Nixon, because it was in the best interest of the country. No one cares that I—and the multitude—suffer from free-floating anxiety because of the state of the union, while our president, the first lady, and members of Congress live and retire in splendor.

---

4.   "News with Brian Williams", Monday, Jan. 9, 2006 (6:30 PM, ET). "Today," Monday, Jan. 9, 2006 (7 AM, ET) msnbc.msn.com (accessed 2/9/2007)

MONEY TALKS IN WASHINGTON

I have no doubt that super-wealthy and well-connected people use their influence to manipulate the government. This has been true since the dawn of America.

The federal government indicted Marc Rich in 1983 on charges of evading more than $48 million in income taxes and illegally buying oil from Iran during the 1979 hostage crisis. He left the United States before the indictment. In 1983, Rich was indicted, but fled to Switzerland before a court appearance. He remained on the FBI's most-wanted list for many years.

William Jefferson Clinton denies that the contribution by Rich's ex-wife to his presidential library motivated him to pardon Marc Rich.[5] The circumstances leave no doubt in my mind that people without any money would not receive a pardon. Think about this. Are voters so stupid as to believe that a person's amoral conduct does not reflect on his ability to govern? In the end, the voters get what they deserve, and we, as a nation, suffer the consequences.

5.   Clinton denies pardon was motivated by money Independent, The (London), Feb 19, 2001 by Mary Dejevsky in Washington,aaa.findarticles.com (accessed 2/9/2007)

3

Pessimism and Optimism

PHILOSOPHICAL OPTIMISM

Optimism is the doctrine that things are getting better and that good will ultimately triumph over evil. But optimists choose to think good thoughts rather than start a revolution against evil. They shy away from thinking about the power of evil and the continuous warfare with it. Since they believe that this is the best of all possible worlds, they have no desire to reform humanity. Instead, they think, "See no evil; hear no evil; speak no evil."

PHILOSOPHICAL PESSIMISM

On the other hand, the pessimist sees only the bad in all things and has no hope that there will be any change. He does not love what he rebukes, and he delights in pointing out faults. Consequently, he is always unhappy.

REVOLUTION AGAINST EVIL

Righteous individuals can see that humanity is in outrageous circumstances and that an all-out war against evil is necessary. Many unrighteous people do not believe that there will be a day of judgment, and they certainly are not interested in declaring war on evil. The righteous are spiritually confident that humanity's restoration to a state of grace is achievable. Unlike optimists, they want to expose the world's evil and reform humanity.

In Ephesians 6:12, St. Paul tells us that we wrestle against principalities, powers, the rulers of the darkness of this world, and spiritual wickedness in high places. Our enemies are invisible, and our main conflict is not with men. Optimists seem unaware of this warfare and play into the hands of the devil when they claim that things on earth are getting better.

HOW TO START A REVOLUTION

First, we need to identify the oppressors and their actions. Second, we need to expose their evil deeds.

As I ponder my statements in this book, I realize that I find fault with our acclaimed institutions and leaders. Furthermore, I am pessimistic that they want to reform humanity. Although I am certain about the institutions that I want to expose, I will not waste more time trying to reform the institutions and leaders. While I will continue to contradict and protest against them, I want to speak the truth to the individuals who pursue truth.

We cannot go off half-cocked when exposing evil. We must not return evil for evil. We will not succeed if we are self-righteous. In other words, remove the concealed evil in your life before you expose the insignificant flaw in someone else's life.

It is essential that you know beforehand the great underlying evil you are to expose. For example, prejudice is one great evil in the world, and it is the cause of war. Prejudice is another form of hate, and love is the cure.

Before you start the revolution, it is essential that you observe the acts of individuals that you have reason to think have prejudice against another race, religion, culture, etc. Chances are that you are such a person. Start a revolution in your life, then you can expose the evil in others.

Let us assume that you are aware of the factors mentioned above. Your victory over evil requires that you know of the principalities, the powers, the rulers of the darkness of this world, and spiritual wickedness in high places. It's one thing to know how to start a revolution, but it is more important to know how to win battles. I keep in mind the following instructions, which I learned from scriptures:

> Pray to God that he allows nothing to be a temptation to you.
> Diligently study and keep the Ten Commandments.
> Know your enemy: people connected with the devil or other powerful destructive forces.
> Know their tactics. They tell lies and they do not believe in scriptures, or they quote scriptures for their purpose.

Know how to counterattack. Obey and quote scriptures, and the devil will flee.
Pursue truth in the scriptures so that you can confront the devil's lies.
Remember that the Holy Spirit abides in you and that the battle is the lord's.
Never lose faith when you encounter the devil.
Believe that the Bible is the word of God.

This book is a part of the revolution I started many years ago. You might be curious about how things are going with me in this regard. I have many battle scars. I have made my share of mistakes. I know a great deal more now than when I started. I have not left the battlefield. To date, I have identified my prison and many of the causes for failure, and I have kept the faith. I am alone in my endeavor, but there are many others in the battle to expose evil.

Jesus is my only source of a way to expose evil in institutions and individuals. The Old Testament revealed to the Jews that they are God's chosen people, and they assumed that no one else was in a covenant relationship with God. Jesus was a revolutionary teacher of a new covenant of love for humanity. The Jews had a prejudice against non-Jews (gentiles). To make matters worse, Jesus boldly told them that the Samaritan was a good neighbor and loved by God. It was absurd to a Jew that God would allow Samaritans to be a part of his chosen people. Jesus told them to love their enemies.

There are numerous evils that should be exposed, and the one Jesus chose to highlight was prejudice, or hatred. This is the evil you too should highlight and expose. Resist the temptation to be politically correct. In a loving way, remind others of the Golden Rule; they do not want others to hate them, so they ought not to hate others. Banish from your thoughts all racial and ethnic slurs, and do not keep company with people who make them. Make it a practice to understand and identify with people of other races and cultures. If you genuinely love God, he will reveal to you the depth of his love for you and all others, regardless of their skin color, culture, sex, or religion.

Prejudice and hatred come in many forms. Christian evangelism does not mean telling others that their gods are false gods; it means telling others about the god revealed in the Bible and about his incarnate son, Jesus. In other words, you are to tell others about your god. Arm-twisting, self-righteousness, bigotry, ill will, and ridicule are forms of hatred. Another subtle form of hatred is shaming and humiliating family members, Christians of other persuasions, or individuals of the opposite sex.

The best way to highlight and expose hatred is to love in word and deed. In 1 Pet. 2:23, St. Peter gives us Christ's example for exposing hatred.

"When he was reviled, he did not revile in return; when he suffered, he did not threaten; but he trusted to him who judges justly."

When and if you will prevail in the revolution is yet to be determined. Meanwhile, love is the only way Jesus used to prevail, and it is the only means for you to use. To illustrate, you can overcome evil by feeding those who steal bread because they're hungry, give your enemy a drink of water if he is thirsty, and welcome a stranger who may be lonely and ignored. Kind words and thoughts may be the most effective way to overcome evil, and the kindest words ever uttered were: "Father, forgive them; for they know not what they do" (Luke 23:34).

Prevailing against evil is not a certainty in this life. Jesus tells us to endure to the end.

4

Good and Evil

The struggle with good and evil is common to every person. We all have our own notions about the devil, self-centeredness, and original sin; nevertheless, we can attain this wisdom and be victorious over sin and the devil.

In order to understand evil, we need to answer some fundamental questions. What is the origin of evil? What is its purpose? Why is it so overwhelming? How can we conquer it?

Before going to college, I knew nothing about the origin of evil except that of Lucifer, the fallen angel who wanted to be like God. He became Satan, the evil one from whom we ask God to deliver us in *The Lord's Prayer*.

After I read Martin Buber's *Good and Evil*[1] a second and third time, I began to understand these principles. Buber is without equal when it comes to translating the language of the Old Testament. He taught philosophy from 1938 to 1951 at the Hebrew University in Jerusalem.

THE PSALMS

The Book of Psalms is a collection of songs, prayers, and poetry in the Old Testament. In most of the psalms, the introductory words found before the first verse attribute it to the psalmist, the author. Although King David did not write all of the psalms, he is given credit for most psalms. King Solomon wrote some of them, in addition to Proverbs. Five centuries before the time of David, Moses wrote some of the earliest psalms.

In some psalms, the psalmist, in the midst of despair, pours out his soul in confession, yet he has praise for his provider and comforter. The psalms take us

---

1.   Martin Buber, *Good and Evil*, (Upper Saddle River, New Jersey: Prentice Hall, 1952).

through the crises and high points of human experience, but they guide us to the praise of a loving creator.

Five Psalms

In *Good and Evil*, Buber discusses five psalms that address the world's struggle with these opposing concepts. After translating these five psalms from the original language, he was able to place them in the proper sequence, so they would complete one another and guide us through transforming experiences to one great insight.

In order to understand God's plan for humankind, we must know these principles thoroughly, otherwise we will not be able to understand our motives, conduct, relationships, love, truth, suffering, or purpose. Our eternal life depends on deliverance from and forgiveness of our evil deeds; consequently, we need to know who will deliver us from them, and we need to know the purpose of evil.

PSALM 12

According to Buber, man introduced the lie into nature, because man is capable of conceiving the truth and then directing a lie against it. In a lie, the spirit rebels against itself. Liars teach men to believe their falsehoods.[2]

It has been my experience that whenever I speak the truth to some individuals who are not receptive, they are offended and they direct a lie against it. Only with time did I, like the psalmists, discover that the mind of God is available to me. If I had not discovered this, then I would be on my own, striving to survive.

Being self-centered, I also have an innate tendency to direct a lie against the truth. When I discovered that I was not God, I yearned for God to draw me to himself so that he would communicate with me. No one should be satisfied to live in darkness and direct lies against the truth. Professor Buber discloses the doom of the lie: "This generation is not opposed to God as speaking lies but as being a lie."[3] He goes on to say, "The lie is temporal and will be swallowed up by time; however, divine truth is from eternity."[4]

I see so many people who acknowledge God's existence but attack his attributes, sovereignty, virtue, trustworthiness, honor, etc. God says that he is the

---

2.   Ibid., p. 7
3.   Ibid., p. 12
4.   Ibid., p. 13

great "I am," but many unrighteous and unbelieving individuals deny the existence of God and of biblical and secular history about the prophets and Jesus.
They deny that Jesus was the incarnate son of God. They reject the intelligent
design of creation.

PSALM 14

In every nation, there is a division between those who do violence and their victims. There is also a division between those who are true to God and those who
are not, and this split exists in every soul. These divisions go unnoticed, but they
become apparent in times of crisis. The psalmists had the assurance of divine support and knew that God would arrange the downfall of evil.

This psalm offers me an insight about the cause of evil; namely, that there are
those who deny God's existence. He will deliver those who are true to him.

> *The fool says in his heart, "There is no God." They are corrupt, they do abomina-
> ble deeds, there is none that does good ... They have all gone astray, they are all
> alike corrupt; there is none that does good, no, not one. There they shall be in great
> terror, for God is with the generation of the righteous.*

Psalms 14: 1, 3, 5

PSALM 82

God's earthly representatives must manifest his righteousness. Specifically, it is
their duty to save the persecuted from those who persecute them. Instead, they
allow social injustice by giving undeserved privileges to powerful people. Because
of their conduct, these men have disregarded God's commandments.

In Psalm 82, the psalmist says that the angels did not rule with justice, and
they gave the oppressors all that they desire. "How long will you judge unjustly
and show partiality to the wicked?" The angels walked beneath the word of the
judge, yet they disregarded it. "They have neither knowledge nor understanding,
they walk about in darkness; all the foundations of the earth are shaken."

This psalm confirms my understanding that appointed leaders are God's servants in the administration of justice, and their failure to do so causes men to live
as animals do. Consequently, God's plan for justice is neglected.

PSALM 73

Psalm 73 is instructive about what will happen to the wicked people who are responsible for the fall of a nation.

> "Truly thou dost set them in slippery places; thou dost make them fall to ruin. How they are destroyed in a moment, swept away utterly by terrors! They are like a dream when one awakes, on awaking you despise their phantoms." (vv 18–20)

The Old Testament prophets continued to warn the Israelites to repent, but many refused to listen. Some people today refuse to repent. Those who do repent have a responsibility to share the good news of the gospel with others.

In Psalm 73, the psalmist comes close to disbelief, as he cannot see that God is very active in this earthly life. "All in vain have I kept my heart clean and washed my hands in innocence. For all the day long, I have been stricken, and chastened every morning."

To the psalmist, God appears to prefer the wicked, and he questions his choice to live a good and honorable life. The psalmist calls on his entire mental capacity in order to know the meaning of this conflict. His faulty perception is part of his trouble.

The psalmist takes his concerns to God. When the lord shows him the true state of the wicked, his spiritual eyes open, and he is illuminated. "Until I went into the sanctuary of God; then I perceived their end. Truly, thou dost set them in slippery places; thou dost make them fall to ruin. How they are destroyed in a moment, swept away utterly by terrors! They are like a dream when one awakes; on awaking, they despise their phantoms."

A change takes place in the psalmist that leads him toward God's presence. His change of heart produces new meaning in what was meaningless for so long. Inner change brought on a change in perception.

PSALM 1

Psalm 1 is the last of five used by Professor Buber for understanding good and evil.

Often, it appeared that my continued efforts to do what was right failed; however, I failed only in the eyes of the men who will be "destroyed in a moment, swept away utterly by terrors" (Psalm 73:19).

Many things I have, I really never wanted. Those things that I do not have, I cannot attain. If circumstances are not right, it is unlikely that I will be blessed (happy, joyous, content). Psalm 1 is about happiness. Although I followed the advice given, I have not yet attained much spiritual blessing. Perhaps my spiritual expectations have been unrealistic. I can only conjecture that I failed to see how blessed I am. I have no reason to believe that Saint Paul was a happy person, and as far as I can discover, Saint Francis was joyful but not ecstatic. All this having been said, let us now consider several verses from Psalm 1.

> Blessed is the man who walks not in the counsel of the wicked, nor stands in the way of sinners, nor sits in the seat of scoffers; but his delight is in the law of the LORD, and on his law he meditates day and night. He is like a tree planted by streams of water, that yields its fruit in its season, and its leaf does not wither. In all that he does, he prospers.(v1–3)

The Balance of Good and Evil

God created both good and evil. When we unite the good and evil urges, we are capable of great love and service.[5]

I understand that God interacts with evil but that it does not affect him. I observe that there are good and evil urges in humans, and they are free to yield to the evil urge or unite it with the good urge so that they love and serve God and one another. God had a purpose for the evil urge. For one thing, it is a way for us to perfect our faith in God and not in ourselves. Also, it causes us to repent. In other words, we are free to sin, and when we do, only God can deliver us. He came to us in the form of a sinless man, and he was crucified for us as an atonement for our transgressions.

I see clearly the purpose of evil in the divine plan. I am in the battle against evil so that others will choose rightly and be united with God. He is holy and cannot unite with evil; he wants evil men to repent and be one with him. I am a part of the divine plan that includes the availability of the grace of God for me and all others who believe.

It is God's nature to love and create. He created man with the same capacity to love and create. He gave us minds and spirits to understand the need for the

---

5.   Ibid., pp. 75, 94–97

good urge and its opposite. God is a free spirit, and he created us with the same capacity; however, God set limits on our freedom to sin. In conclusion, God gave us the freedom of choice because he wanted us to love him and one another without compulsion.

This is not an easy concept to understand. I recommend that you study this chapter carefully. A comprehension of good and evil will help you solve the mysteries of who God is and who you are. Without this wisdom, you cannot find the source of power to resist evil and to serve the absolute god. To understand the chapters that follow, you will need spiritual insight, and it is available to anyone with a pure and repentant heart.

All of us yearn to be all that God intended for us to be. When we rely only on our understanding, we are not equipped to live in the world or in the declining American culture.

OUR RESPONSIBILITY

It is not enough to accept the path God reveals. We must cling to it with a passion. We must study the scriptures and follow their living word, the lord Jesus Christ, so that we speak their truths anew today.

5

What is truth?

The decline of American culture is a threat to our integrity and our very survival. I believe there is one question that is fundamental. Pontius Pilate posed the same question to Jesus Christ two thousand years ago when Christ was on trial.

> *Pilate said to him, "So you are a king?"*
> *Jesus answered, "You say that I am a king. For this, I was born, and for this, I have come into the world, to bear witness to the truth. Everyone who is of the truth hears my voice."*
> *Pilate said to him, "What is truth?"*

John 18:37–38

When I entered college in 1948, I asked the question, "What is truth?" Since that time, I have earnestly searched for the answer. In 1966, I intensified my search for the answer, in the hope that it would set me free from my bondage in the American culture. Recently, I started to write my answer to the question, and I have found that my understanding of truth is limited by the lies I was taught to believe.

When we swear to tell the truth and nothing but the truth, we think that we know what truth is and that we have the capability to tell the truth. How is it that twelve people can witness an event and, under oath, give twelve different versions of the event?

What is Truth?

I asked the above question of a person who thinks of himself as one who lives by the truth, yet he was at a loss for words to define it. You too might have difficulty defining it.

One evening, I was trying to come to terms with truth, and suddenly, truth came to terms with me. My perception changed, and I discovered that truth is not mortal, earthly, or a code of conduct. How could I have been so dense that I did not see it before? I had always thought that truth was reality, credibility, verity, actuality, correctness, trustworthiness, integrity, honor, and honesty. Yes, it is all of these, but authentic truth is so much more.

It finally dawned on me that truth is the eternal spirit. Truth is God almighty. I yearn for the truth, the way, and the life, and triune God yearns for me. I now see truth (God) in a glass, darkly, but when I die, I will see truth face to face.

The truth that I so diligently sought elsewhere I found the very first time I believed that God in Christ is the truth, the way, and the life. The truth dwells in me. There is no place to go to find truth. I already have the capacity to see and receive it. If there is anything that remains to be done, then I must constantly remind myself that truth sets free those who seek it. I repeat that God is the truth.

> *If you love me, you will keep my commandments. And I will pray the Father, and he will give you another Counselor, to be with you forever, even the Spirit of truth, whom the world cannot receive, because it neither sees him nor knows him; you know him, for he dwells with you, and will be in you.*

John 14:15–17

A lie is an intentional misstatement, fabrication, deception, false swearing, or perjury. The lie is not mortal, earthly, or a code of conduct. A lie is an evil spirit that also dwells in humans. That spirit rebelled against God, his creator. In addition, there are wicked spirits at God's command to execute his will against the wicked. "Now the spirit of the lord departed from Saul, and an evil spirit from the lord tormented him" (1 Samuel 16:14).

In summary, it is helpful to understand that we are fighting against the world rulers of this present darkness and against the spiritual hosts of wickedness in the heavenly places (Eph. 6:12).

We will not know God until he reveals himself to us. Then we shall know the truth.

ABSOLUTE TRUTH

Webster's New World College Dictionary defines truth as "the quality of being in accordance with experience, facts, or reality; actual existence." The ancient Greek word for truth is *aletheia*. It had several meanings in the New Testament. Depending on the context in which it is used, it means "trustworthiness," "certainty," "honesty," or "reality."

Webster's New World College Dictionary defines "absolute" as "ultimate reality regarded as uncaused, unmodified, unified and complete, and timeless."

The carnal mind is in conflict with the spiritual mind; it needs to unite with the spiritual in order to see and comprehend the spirit of truth. Each of them has a different function, in the same way as the bad and the good urge. Individuals must unite them to serve God with all their hearts.

RELATIVE TRUTH

Protagoras, an ancient Greek mathematician and philosopher, claimed that truth is not an absolute and that all values and judgments are relative. According to Protagoras, each individual has a personal understanding of truth, and no one has an ultimate truth.

Socrates argued that Protagoras' theory is an absolute that denies the existence of absolutes. He dismissed Protagoras' theory as absurd.

CAN WE CHOOSE A LIE?

My experience has shown me that almost all people believe lies at one time or another. Life offers one illusion after another. For example, disparities of income and wealth are growing more in the United States than in other nations. Our legislators would have the low-income citizens believe that politicians are doing everything necessary to solve the problem. This is a misrepresentation or a bold-faced lie. Poverty is increasing, not decreasing.

Furthermore, democracy, as we have known it, is a web of lies and deception. Voters believe the lying politicians who say things that make voters feel comfortable and require no effort on their part; yet voters ignore the truth-telling politicians who say things voters do not want to hear and would rather not think about. The war in Iraq is a painful example. The Bush administration claims that the United States is making progress in Iraq, but there is evidence that more servicemen are dying every month. One political party provides facts that totally contradict the other party. Which version is true? The soul pledges itself to the truth or to the lie. When we choose a lie instead of truth, we fall victim to it. This choice is a decision of the soul and does not attest to the truth or falsehood of the things themselves.

THE SEARCH FOR TRUTH

I recently read a book entitled *Truth: A History and a Guide for the Perplexed* by Felipe Fernandez-Armesto.[1] Armesto has been a member of the modern history faculty of Oxford University since 1983. He claims that our society has lost faith in the reality of truth and lost interest in the search for it. He reviews the history of the concept of truth in order to explain how we got into these predicaments, and he suggests clues about what might happen next. He writes about truth in society, not about individual thoughts concerning truth.

I draw heavily on Armesto's ideas, because he knows far more about truth in society than I know. I did a lot of research on the subject, because I wanted to know about genuine truth. After analyzing other authorities and Armesto's and comparing them with mine, I found that Armesto's was more complete. In his last chapter, entitled "Life after Doubt," Armesto asserts that Protagoras's principle of relativism is difficult to ignore.

> Protagoras fits cozily into a world of demolished orthodoxies in which anything goes. He is distinctly audible above the information explosion, which disables disagreement by making it impossible for anyone to be entirely sure of his subject.[2]

Relativism in America allows anyone to express an opinion and claim that it is relative truth.

---

1. Felipe Fernandez-Armesto, *Truth: A History and a Guide for the Perplexed* (New York: St. Martin's Griffin, 2001).

2. Ibid., p. 205.

TOLERANCE

To most of us, tolerance means that everyone has a right to his own opinion. We can acknowledge views, beliefs, and practices that differ from our own without agreeing or sympathizing with them. Frankly, I cannot comprehend what a relativist uses to determine what is right and what is wrong, other than personal preference. As far as I know, a relativist lives by personal preferences that he or she believes are correct. Those who make these claims consider all opinions equally valid. This being the case, they want equal protection under the law to live the lives they choose.

The fact that a relativist does not believe in absolutes does not mean that he or she cannot be a law-abiding and trustworthy person, nor does it mean that he or she condones evil. But it is apparent to me that relativism makes it impossible for anyone to be entirely sure about anything, including good and evil.

Thanks to the advertising, entertainment, and broadcasting media, liberal tolerance and relativism infest the minds and spirits of Americans who choose the anything-goes lifestyle.

For one who believes in the god of the Bible, tolerance based on moral relativism is impossible. Because the relativists do not believe in absolutes, we cannot resolve social, political, and value conflicts by reason or compromise.

Here again, there is a kind of personal preference in the world of relative theology. As for me, I am willing to argue with a professional theologian on such issues as unconditional love, blessing same-sex marriages, and the like, so long as we agree on a monotheistic god—father, son, and holy ghost—and that the Bible is the inerrant word of God.

Christians are not supposed to be tolerant of wickedness; however, the Bible makes it clear that "to set the mind on the flesh is death, but to set the mind on the Spirit is life and peace" (Romans 8:6–7).

Relativists insist that all conduct, whether theirs or that of others, moral or immoral, is neither right nor wrong and is therefore acceptable. In other words, there are no absolutes by which to decide what is right or wrong. But Christian love does not mean that we must approve relativism or any conduct that is contrary to Christian doctrine.

RESCUING TRUTH FROM "RELATIVIZATION"

I imagine that before the origin of language, humankind lived by whatever it was that we later named truth. After the origin of language, humans named truth and its opposite, falsehood. They named good and its opposite, evil. Humans were free to choose between good and evil. I also imagine that humankind did not always agree on the meaning of truth and falsehood.

Essentially, humankind has lived in chaos since its creation. Individuals, civilizations, and America were born in chaos. Meanwhile, how shall we live, and what for? This leads me to consider Armesto's truth-finding techniques, which will reveal how to live a righteous life and survive in what I named a declining culture. The techniques will answer Pontius Pilate's question, "What is truth?"

FINDING TRUTH

In his book, Armesto provides four categories of truth-finding techniques. They are tradition, consensus, reason and sense perception, and objectivity. Armesto suggests we can turn back to tradition or chase away subjectivism and relativism until truth prevails. Remembering what past generations learned is the foundation for what is genuine truth for us today.[3]

TRADITION

Armesto discusses the use of instincts by our ancestors. Consciousness changes our alertness to danger, hunger, and fear (instincts) into inner feelings that can be a truth-telling method that is not necessarily subjective but can be deceptive. Our instincts must be tested by other techniques, because they cannot always be distinguished from other feelings that may be entirely subjective. I use this technique in conjunction with reason and sense perception. Even then, I do not know with certainty when others are untrustworthy. Nowadays, many people know the truth and choose to disregard it, so I use this technique with caution. For example, when Lyndon Johnson heard a man claim that he was "just an old country boy," Johnson instinctively put his hand on his wallet, because he felt that the man might be a liar—up to no good.

---

3.   Ibid., pp. 217–220.

IMPOSED BY CONSENSUS OR ENFORCED BY AUTHORITY

According to Armesto, claims made by those in authority carry only a presumption in their favor, not a guarantee of truth. They cannot be trusted on their own. If an authority confirms what I thought to be the truth, then I am supported.

I agree with an authority's enforcement of truth. I abide by the rule of law, even when it is different from what I feel to be true. But on some occasions, legislative and judicial authorities have enforced laws in violation of the Constitution. The U.S. internment of citizens of Japanese origin is one example. Another example is the 1896 case of *Plessy v. Ferguson*.[4] The Supreme Court ruled that separate but equal schools for African Americans was lawful. In *Brown v. Board of Education of Topeka*,[5] the Supreme Court reversed *Plessy v. Ferguson*. The consensus technique does have its flaws.

REASON AND SENSE PERCEPTION

According to Armesto, reason and sense perception provide truths that strengthen each other; they are not necessarily incompatible with the transcendent truth. In conjunction with reason and perception, we are well advised to take instruction from the truth we feel and are told.

In my opinion, our creator gifted us with reason, sense perception, and the freedom to use or to ignore them. Reason is subject to human error, and logic is not perfect, but both are performed by instinctive minds and conscientious thinking. I rely on reason and sense perception most. When I am in doubt, I rely on my sixth sense, the indwelling Holy Spirit.

OBJECTIVITY

Objectivity is a compilation of subjective views, and it is elusive. We can only rely on the written or oral statements of others and unconfirmed reports. It is impossible to see from every point of view, and it is absurd to see from no point of view.[6]

---

4.   Plessy v Ferguson, 163 U.S. 537 (1896).
5.   *Brown v. Board of Education of Topeka*, 347 U.S. 483 (1954).

Armesto does not say whether objectivity will lead us to truth. A subjective statement of fact may not be a universal truth in the sense that it is correct for all times and places; nevertheless, it behooves us to be willing to listen to a subjective view and determine if it is true.

Jesus said, "I am the way, and the truth, and the life; no one comes to the Father, but by me" (John 14:6). His claim is correct for all times and places. Jesus Christ is the same yesterday and today and forever (Hebrews 13:8). It is the Holy Spirit that makes Christ real and present in my life now.

The historical Christ whom I know now is the Christ I will know and enjoy forever. His statement in John 14:6 is objective truth and corresponds to the object: truth.

Absolute truth is true regardless of what I believe and think, and it is true for all people, at all times and in all places. It stands on its own, no matter what evidence there is for it.

I cannot find God ("absolute truth") until he reveals himself. Thereafter, I can find partial "absolute" truth about him by using reason and logic; however, it is beyond my finite ability to find the ultimate source of absolute truth.

The psalmists did not find answers to their conflicts until they changed their perception. We too need go into the sanctuary of the lord and change our perception, so that the lord will reveal the truth to us.

SACRED

Truth can come from an unheard voice within, the source of which is God himself—the great "I am."

HOW TO RELY ON JESUS TO DISCERN TRUTH

Someone asked me how it is that I rely on Jesus to discern truth. After a moment of thought, I realized that the question was ambiguous; it could mean "why?", or it could mean "what caused me to rely on Jesus?" There is another possible meaning of the question, and that is "how do I go to Jesus?" Nevertheless, I endeavored to answer the question as I understood it.

The trinity is the father, the son (Jesus), and the Holy Spirit (counselor) that dwells within me. Although I use the techniques suggested by Armesto, I rely

---

6.   Ibid., p. 228.

more on the Holy Spirit to witness to my spirit and guide me to the truth. The scriptures revealed this technique to me.

This technique should not be strange to a mature Christian, because he is in constant communion with the spirit in all matters. That does not mean that he is not conscious of the physical world. He is capable of functioning in the world and paying attention to his inner counselor at the same time.

The Bible is the word of God, and the words of Jesus are recorded there. His commandments are there. His parables and the gospels instruct me how to live by faith and not by sight. By faith through grace, I am led into all truth. From the Bible, I learned about justice, love, charity, compassion, mercy, forgiveness, moderation, thankfulness, redemption, evil, and the seven deadly sins and virtues, among other things. The techniques mentioned by Armesto were not my primary source of truth.

The spirit counsels me to engage in communion with the body of Christ, the Church. God uses other learned Christians to teach scriptures to me and to give guidance about my secular and spiritual activities.

The saints of God provide a tangible example of the way the spirit perfects those who are obedient to the will of God. Their prayers, temptations, devotions, suffering, and confessions revealed truth to me.

I discover my duty by using Jesus' doctrine and example. I obtain my happiness because of his merit and intercession. I receive God's blessings through Jesus. I can come to God by repentance and by acts of worship, due to Christ's spirit and grace. I obtain the happiness of coming to God because of Christ's merit and righteousness.

The bread and cup of the Lord's Supper are two symbols that have unique definite meanings that summarize the entire Christian life. The bread represents the Old Testament, and the cup represents the New Testament. Every scripture pertaining to my walk with the lord can be seen as relating to the bread, to the cup, or to both. Meditate on the words spoken by a minister prior to offering the bread and the cup:

> The lord Jesus, on the night when he was betrayed, took bread; and when he had given thanks, he broke it, and said, "This is my body, which is for you. Do this in remembrance of me." In the same way also he took the cup, after supper, saying, "This cup is the new covenant in my blood. Do this, as often as you drink it, in remembrance of me." For as often as you eat this bread and drink the cup, you proclaim the lord's death until he comes.

About twenty years ago, by divine providence, I discovered the ancient practice of meditation. In the Catholic tradition, it is called Christian contemplative prayer. It is a prayer of silence in which I experience God's presence by opening my mind and heart to God.

Contemplation was the only way for me to stop my brain chatter in a life full of endless desires and suffering. In addition to engaging in silent prayer, I studied world religions. The Buddhist religion provided evidence that desire is one cause of suffering. This truth uncovered the cause for my dissatisfaction with materialism, which promotes a life of excess, with the attendant suffering.

Contemplation gives a new dimension to prayer and worship. Mysticism and silence gives a new dimension to life. I often wonder why the Protestant religion has not joined the Christian contemplative heritage. I would hazard to guess that during the Reformation, the reformers discarded *lectio divina* (praying the scriptures) and other Catholic traditions, including private confession. My spiritual life would have been more fruitful if I had included *lectio divina* and private confession.

In all matters, secular and sacred, I rely on faith and use my God-given intelligence to know the truth. I use reason and faith to understand the scriptures. I know that without the grace of God, I am capable of committing every sin.

The extremist and the nihilist are opposed to the foregoing concepts, and the subjectivists can only speak with reasonable certainty.[7]

There is no option but to search for truth. Truth is divinely ordained. Our souls yearn after truth. Our nation is in decline because too many Americans yearn after sensual pleasure, and as with the wicked, so is it with the nation. "The truth-quest is always the same: the unwavering search for signs to match reality."[8]

Jesus identifies an underlying cause why the wicked do not search for signs to match reality. As I will explain in greater detail later on, the wicked do not search for truth. They have nothing to do with the truth, because there is no truth in them. Jesus described the devil as a liar and the father of lies. Every day, we encounter individuals who have evil motives and tell lies to perpetuate their desires. Hitler and Stalin are two examples of this.

---

7.   Felipe Fernandez-Armesto, *Truth: A History and a Guide for the Perplexed* (New York: St. Martin's Griffin, 2001), pp. 223–226.

8.   Ibid., p. 227.

EXPERIENCING TRUTH

Until I experience a particular truth, I cannot know its trustworthiness; however, I am capable of experiencing its trustworthiness without tangible evidence. For example, I have experienced the reality and manifestations of God.

If you read between the lines, you will probably recognize that I encountered a lot of struggles, and I have not mentioned the majority of them. Suffering is not an illusion. To me, most Americans do not seem to be bothered about the evil state of this nation; in fact, they appear to enjoy the desires of the flesh. How long do you think American culture will survive the irresponsible drinking of alcohol, substance abuse, adultery, and fornication that you observe?

I have witnessed success and failure, poverty and wealth, truth and lies, justice and injustice, self-centeredness and self-renunciation, charity and greed, and moral and immoral conduct. There were times when I was optimistic and times when I was pessimistic. There were times when I had no remedy for the plight of those who were suffering.

Through it all, I found no philosophy, no psychology, no refuge, and no culture that provided meaning to the madness. I found no deliverance from the everyday variety of evil other than God incarnate in Jesus Christ. In the depth of my despair, I had calmness and a genuine refuge that I had never before encountered. I found nobody—no institution, no culture, and no nation—that offered any truth greater than Jesus: the way, the truth, and the life.

I am confident that I know the meaning of and purpose for my suffering. I am now bold enough to confront evil, without fear of any consequences. My spiritual life is not as complicated, and my theology has been reduced to loving God and all things he created, and rejoicing in the truth.

OUR RESPONSIBILITY

Truth is a gift of God, who is the possessor and the giver of all truth. By the power of the Holy Spirit, truth can come to the light of our awareness. Such truth liberates us from doubts, illusions, and fears (see John 8:32).

The more profound the truth we experience, the more complete our freedom will be. The deeper the truth we come to know, the more complete our liberation. To find absolute truth is to find absolute freedom.

6

Truth and Falsehood

All day long, lies bombard me.

"Your call is important to us."

"Our technicians are busy helping other customers. Someone will be with you shortly."

"Lose thirty pounds in two weeks or your money back—guaranteed."

I spend hours on the phone listening to such nonsense, and I read junk mail filled with similar drivel. There is simply no other word to describe it but hogwash. *Webster's New World College Dictionary* defines "hogwash" as "nonsense."

Liars dominate American culture, and they make lies appear as truths. Liars are in government, businesses, corporations, and educational institutions. Even private citizens try to convince us to believe their falsehoods. Lies come forth from them as spontaneous expressions of experience and insight. They speak "great things" and thereby attempt to bind us to them.

TO THINE OWN SELF BE TRUE

In William Shakespeare's *Hamlet*, Polonius eloquently advises Laertes, "This above all: to thine own self be true, and it must follow, as the night the day, thou canst not then be false to any man."[1] In Jeremiah 17:9, we read, "The heart is deceitful above all things, and desperately corrupt; who can understand it?" I have read these lines many times before, but I did not grasp the totality of the message they convey until the moment was right, and then they came to mind.

I am acquainted with several individuals who are selfish, irresponsible, and not true to themselves. Their irresponsible demands are a burden and an irritation. Every time they do not have their way, they pout and create a disturbance that shames and humiliates others. In addition, they have no remorse for their mis-

---

1.   William Shakespeare's Hamlet, Act I scene III, (C.f., WilliamShakespeare.com)

conduct, falsely accuse others of wrongdoing, and vindictively damage others' reputations. In addition to deceiving themselves, they deceive others. They choose to accuse their adversaries of lying rather than admit that they are liars. They deny that there is any possibility that they are wrong. They do all this in order to cover up negative character traits and neglect of responsibility. They give a false account of events that have caused conflict, and people believe them. They believe that they are righteous. Needless to say, such individuals try men's souls.

ANGEL OF LIGHT

I have said a great deal about how to know Jesus, but I have said nothing that will help you identify Satan, the enemy of our souls. I never saw him in a red leotard with horns on his brow, or in bodily form. I have seen his sinister apparition in humans, animals (mad dogs), drug users, alcoholics, religious impostors, adulterers, fornicators, drunks, sexual perverts, murderers, and the like.

Satan masquerades as an angel of light, and his servants masquerade as servants of righteousness. Only Satan would plan the extermination of millions. Hitler and Stalin were pawns in the hands of the devil. In recent times, Saddam Hussein, Idi Amin (the "Butcher of Uganda"), and Slobodan Milosevic were evil and did evil.

Many Christians believe that there is a devil, but some conveniently forget it or fail to remember their propensity for evil. Some are rarely truthful to themselves, and from time to time, they lie to others.

There are nominal Christians who masquerade as angels of light. Their cruel self-righteous words, thoughts, and deeds cause irreparable harm to their families and to other innocent victims. At times, the devil is their prime mover, and a great deal of the time, it is their propensity to sin.

ANALYZING HOGWASH

When I began working on this chapter, I assumed that there were no written analyses of the topic. Then I discovered a book called *On Bullshit*,[2] written by Harry G. Frankfurt, a professor of philosophy at Princeton University. He confirmed my opinion that falsehoods permeate every aspect of American culture.

---

2.   Harry G. Frankfurt, *On Bullshit* (Princeton University Press, 2005).

Professor Frankfurt identified two types of liars: the bullshitter (hereafter refered to as "hogwasher" and the deceiver.

According to Professor Frankfurt, the hogwasher lacks concern for truth. He may not intend to deceive, but since he pays no attention to truth, he misrepresents his intentions. The hogwasher is a greater enemy of the truth than the deceiver is.

Furthermore, the hogwasher's focus is not on the facts. He selects them or makes them up to suit his purpose. These individuals speak with presumed authority on subjects about which they have little, if any, knowledge.[3]

On the other hand, a deceiver starts with a truth and then fabricates subtle and believable lies under the guise of that truth. A liar is devious, two-faced, and untrustworthy.[4]

Based on the professor's account, I conclude that President Bush and his administration did not willfully make statements they knew were untrue; therefore, they do not fit the definition of deceivers. They negligently made statements to serve their purposes. The director of the CIA, without reliable evidence, told President Bush that Iraq had weapons of mass destruction. The president allegedly relied on the director's assurances and sent American troops into Iraq. Then Secretary of State Colin Powell told the United Nations that there was reliable evidence that Iraq was supporting al-Qaeda. Congress, the cabinet, several governmental agencies, and many U.S. citizens supported the president's decision. The president changed his battle cry from "War on terrorism" to "Free Iraq."

I also conclude that President Clinton, in the Lewinsky matter, fits the definition of a deceiver. He wanted the Lewinsky scandal behind him, so he covered it up with a lie that he did not have sex with "that woman." He wanted Americans to believe something he knew to be false.

HOGWASH: THE AMERICAN WAY

Business

In order to survive in competitive America, individuals and institutions incorporate false rhetoric into their advertisements. Public relations firms are masters of twisting the truth. They prepare brochures, ads, and other marketing material that is loaded with untruths, and then they charge their clients—even nonprofit

---

3.   Ibid., pp. 47–54
4.   Ibid., pp. 51, 54–55

corporations, churches, universities, professionals, pharmaceutical companies, and manufacturers—substantial fees for their services.

Job applicants commonly exaggerate their work experience and skills. For example, they may claim the title of president yet have limited experience in management. Many employment consultants encourage this practice.

Politics

Clever people can cover up a lie by mixing it with an ounce of truth. In political circles, this is "spin." According to news commentator Chris Matthews, a person admits that she or he has a problem, thereby establishing credibility. She or he uses that enhanced credibility to define the problem in a way that keeps the political damage to a minimum.[5]

In my opinion, dirty ads and smear tactics are now the standard for political campaigns. Rather than attempt to distinguish them, I feel safe in identifying them as hogwash. Neither party provides positive solutions for problems. Instead, they spend an exorbitant amount of money conducting dishonest hogwash campaigns.

Come Inauguration Day, the president-elect has no shame about the brainless promises he made. He is ill qualified for the office that he obtained by questionable means.

Social Life

Most Americans have opinions about everything that pertains to their country's affairs. Whenever a person's opportunities to speak about some topic exceed his knowledge of relevant facts, hogwash is the natural result. Most people speak extensively about topics of which they are, at least to some degree, ignorant.

THE LIE DEFINED

Webster's New World College Dictionary lists the following synonyms for the verb "lie": falsify, prevaricate, fib, equivocate, fabricate, deceive, mislead, misinform, misrepresent, exaggerate, distort, misstate, misspeak, concoct, forswear, dupe, pervert, slant, twist, overstate, embellish, overdraw, bear false witness, say one thing and mean another, dissimulate, dissemble, perjure oneself, delude, malign,

---

5.   Chris Matthews, *How Politics Is Played, Told by One Who Knows the Game*, (New York: Simon & Schuster, 1999).

invent, manufacture, make up, trump up, palter, beguile, tell a white lie, stretch the truth, spin a long yarn.

Most of us frequently engage in one or more of the acts included in the definition of "lie." We do not give much thought to spinning a long yarn, telling a white lie, or exaggerating. Sometimes I exaggerate in order to be humorous or to emphasize a point. If we intend to deceive people when we say one thing and mean another, we are liars. When we do not know the subject under discussion and give the impression that our statements have merit, then we are deceitful. In short, we are treading on dangerous ground.

Jesus identifies an underlying cause for individuals to reject the truth, to believe a lie, and to teach others to believe a lie. A lie is an impersonation of the truth. It is a wolf in sheep's clothing. Jesus described the devil as a liar and the father of lies: "You are of your father the devil, and your will is to do your father's desires. He was a murderer from the beginning, and has nothing to do with the truth, because there is no truth in him. When he lies, he speaks according to his own nature, for he is a liar and the father of lies" (John 8:44).

DECEIT IS A SERIOUS MATTER

Lies caused the fall of Adam, the crucifixion of Jesus, the extermination of millions, the decline of civilizations, and the torment and suffering of individuals from the beginning of recorded history. Maybe this line of reasoning is not obvious, but lies are the underlying cause of the deaths of American sons and daughters in Iraq, the impeachment of President Clinton, the mishandling of emergency relief to New Orleans, and a multitude of serious disagreements between people and the government and one another.

THE FIRST LIE

In the book of Genesis, God told Adam that he would surely die if he ate fruit from the tree of knowledge. Satan told Adam that he would not die if he ate that fruit. Unfortunately, Adam believed the lie. Many of our ancestors have exercised their free will and opted to believe the first lie ever told to humankind: that they can be like God.

THE ULTIMATE LIE

When Satan entered into Judas, he accused Jesus falsely and conspired with the chief priests about how they might put Jesus to death. Death followed a false accusation. Judas betrayed Jesus with a kiss. Although Jesus foresaw his betrayal, I imagine that he suffered agony when Judas drew near to betray him. Judas was a murderer and a liar, just like Satan.

Most of us can relate to what Jesus suffered. Christians often make false accusations about fellow believers, with no apparent thought for the consequences. Friends or family members may betray us with feigned love. Someone may have swindled you into believing a lie, and you may have passed on that lie to others unwittingly.

EVERYONE LIES SOMETIMES

People lie for a number of reasons. Some lie out of pride or jealousy. In Matthew 27:17–18, we read that the Pharisees handed Jesus over to Pilate out of envy. Others lie because they want to gain an advantage over another person. Those who take credit for something they do not deserve are lying. People who hate tell lies out of revenge.

People lie to cover up shortcomings. They make commitments or promises and do not keep them. They blame others and shift responsibility from themselves.

Many lie because they are afraid to take responsibility for their words and actions. For instance, Nixon, Clinton, G. W. Bush, and members of Congress told lies rather than admit criminal acts and suffer the consequences. Deceit is rampant and will ultimately cause the fall of American culture. Private citizens do not have a way or the means to prosecute the accused; consequently, they suffer the loss of sons and daughters in a needless and costly war.

COMBATING FALSEHOOD

Hogwash requires a listener. If you refuse to listen, the hogwasher will not be successful in his con game. We should not accept lying and deception as the norm. When honest citizens or religious icons consort with elected representatives and fail to protest against lying and blatant immorality in public office, they become accomplices. Religious institutions become irrelevant when the members do not protest against leaders engaged in unethical and ruthless grasps for power and control.

Individuals have the responsibility to protest against the moral corruption of educational institutions that allow students to engage in substance abuse, sexual assaults, cheating on examinations, and unjustifiably demanding higher grades.

OUR RESPONSIBILITY

We must test whether any proposition is true or false; however, degenerates are not reliable enough to perform such a test. Each of us has a false self and a true self, a carnal self and a spiritual self.

Continuous internal warfare occurs in our souls between the flesh and the spirit. We cannot always distinguish whose voice we hear. Sometimes we choose to believe a lie; other times, we are blind to the truth. Not only must we be aware of this duality, we must be on guard, so that we may distinguish between the carnal mind and the spiritual mind. Fortunately, with practice, this is not difficult. But you cannot know the truth about spiritual matters until you receive the embodiment of truth: Jesus. In addition, you cannot know God until you experience Jesus. It is the function of the Holy Spirit to bear witness to your spirit about spiritual truth.

Our battle with Satan, the father of lies, creates anxiety, frustration, and anger. His lies are the primary cause of the imminent decline of America and the spiritual death of many. Nevertheless, Jesus Christ, the embodiment of truth, is able to free us, if we allow him.

7

Between Two Evils

American theologian Tryon Edwards (1809–1894) said, "Between two evils, choose neither; between two goods, choose both."[1]

In the United States, we have two political parties from which to choose: Democrats and Republicans. Unfortunately, we do not have two good things from which to choose; rather, there are two evils. Both liberals and conservatives want to maintain the status quo and power in Congress. Each party gives lip service to the conditions in America, but few, if any, politicians on either side really do anything about it.

No American political party has been free of corruption. During the past ten years, both parties have played the blame game, focusing their efforts on discrediting the opposing party. Politicians seem to be more interested in reelection than in the welfare of their fellow citizens. I have no confidence that this will change.

Nowadays, few people are qualified for the job of president. Any one born in America can grow up to be the president of the United States, but those who are truly qualified have little chance to become president. As it is with almost every other powerful position, money is the name of the game.

In the 2004 presidential debates, two rich and incompetent Yale alumni ran for president. Neither candidate provided honest, intelligent answers to the issues at hand; instead, they focused on discrediting their opponent. They gave us a choice between two evils.

The seven deadly sins and bureaucracy are the root causes of corruption in government. The poor are getting poorer because neither party has the integrity, willingness, aptitude, or expertise to solve the problem of poverty. Revenue from high-bracket and middle-income taxpayers is squandered on war games and mindless deficit spending. Elected representatives appropriate billions for foreign

---

1. Brainyquote.com, s.v. "Tryon Edwards," http://www.brainyquote.com/quotes/quotes/t/tryonedwar126243.html (accessed Sept 20, 2006).

aid and cry out about human rights violations in foreign countries, but they do little to alleviate poverty in America.

Individuals are helpless to solve domestic and international problems. The ballot box has been the only avenue for change. The political despair could not be more obvious. I received a telephone call from a woman pleading with me to listen to a recorded message from Newt Gingrich, who spoke on behalf of an unknown conservative organization. He blamed the Republican leadership in Washington for the lost control of Congress, and he assured me that the conservatives would regain control. I hung up before the woman could read a prepared solicitation for money.

Moments ago, I received another call from a conservative group, asking for my impression of the State of the Union address and offering a message about the Whitewater scandal. I gave her an earful and hung up.

Yesterday, on the front page, there was a picture of Nancy Pelosi with her cheesy grin, gloating about Democratic victories. I want to know if Nancy or Hillary believes that the members of their old girls club are less wicked than members of the old boys club. I would be pleased if women had the opportunity to run the country; then we could evaluate if they are the righteous ones who will deliver us from evil.

Televised kickboxing from Las Vegas is mild compared with the smear campaigns I expect in the future. Between these two evils, I choose neither, hoping that the demise of the corrupt two parties will accelerate. I have enough struggles in fighting off their leader, the devil.

THE TWO-PARTY SYSTEM

Democrats seem to be more liberal in appropriating funds for social welfare in order to help the lower-income class. The Republicans appear to be more conservative in their interpretation of the Constitution as it relates to the separation of church and state and the right to bear arms. But Republicans are not necessarily members of the wealthy upper class, and Democrats are not always members of the lower or middle classes.

Voters in the South and the Midwest tend to be more conservative, and the voters in the metropolitan areas of the East and West tend to be more liberal. Labor unions support the Democrats, and big business supports the Republicans.

Both parties would have citizens believe that they are bipartisan, but the elected representatives will vote the party line in order to gain political advantage. Bipartisanism is an illusion.

VOTING CORRUPTION

When I lived in West Virginia, on one election day, I witnessed a Democratic Party worker, the mother of my grade-school friend, standing near the polling place with a large stack of one-dollar bills. She handed two dollars and a marked ballot to each of numerous black voters. A short time after they voted, I saw the bribed voters intoxicated on cheap rye whiskey purchased from the state store. (State employees were largely Democrats in West Virginia during that time.)

I believe that Republican politicians are equally as corrupt as Democrats. For many decades in West Virginia, few Republican candidates prevailed in statewide elections. The West Virginia presidential primary provided strong momentum for the election of John F. Kennedy.

The labor unions' endorsement of candidates distresses me. It is shameful that unions and corporations contribute huge sums to the political parties they believe will support their economic interests. They also pressure their dues-paying members to vote for particular candidates. Lobbyists for private interest groups do not serve the will of the American people. If money and influence are so sought after and needed for the success of elected officials, it is reasonable to conclude that the holder of a purse can influence the majority to elect the candidates who will reward their efforts. There are loopholes in the law that governs campaign contributions, and neither party sees fit to enact more restrictive laws. The candidate with the largest war chest has a better chance of being elected. Costly campaign ads influence people to vote for a named candidate. One would be naïve to believe that we live in a righteous nation.

DEMOCRATS' AND REPUBLICANS' OPINIONS ABOUT POVERTY

The class system and political system go hand in glove with our form of government. Both parties give lip service to reducing poverty, and they appeal to members of the poor working class to vote for their respective party candidates. Each party bribes the voters with a promise that they will enact legislation to provide greater benefits to the poor. Political parties have expressed opinions on poverty from the date the Constitution was adopted to the present time. It is a fact that the poor have been getting poorer since then, while the politicians have been getting richer.

Poverty is sort of a labor management issue. The poor are analogous to labor, and the rich are analogous to management. In order for the poor to rise above their state, management must pay higher wages. From time to time, the hourly minimum wage is increased to benefit the poor; however, management increases the costs of their product in order to offset the costs of production.

Taxes are increased to offset the cost of benefits for the poor, inflation, and increases in costs for governmental services and defense. Critical eyes can see that financial needs increase at every level. The poverty line today is equal to the compensation that was paid to a United States senator approximately forty years ago. Unfortunately, the increased cost of living is such that a middle-class family of four is barely getting by. Despite what the parties tell the voters and despite the poverty bills that are enacted, the poor are getting poorer.

In 2001, the Kaiser Family Foundation and Harvard University's Kennedy School of Government found that attitudes about poverty and welfare were evenly split along party lines. The study showed that Democrats were more willing to support programs for the poor and Republicans were more likely to support programs where beneficiaries would learn to help themselves; Republicans were less likely to support raising taxes toward this end.[2]

CORPORATE ECONOMY

Some companies (and their owners) have become wealthy by exploiting immigrants or outsourcing jobs overseas. Millions of illegal immigrants are doing work that American citizens will not do for the wages offered. Since products made in foreign lands are less expensive, consumers do not boycott them.

Cheap overseas labor is taking away work from our citizens. The cost of labor in the United States is forcing small businesses to close and large corporations to outsource jobs in order to stay competitive. A growing number of the working poor can only afford to shop at stores like Wal-Mart, whose goods are priced artificially low because they are mostly made in China.

---

2.   "Poverty in America" an NPR/Kaiser/Kennedy School Poll, National Public Radio, Washington, D.C. (2001).

CAUSES OF POVERTY

A poor man cannot acquire wealth, because he does not have the financial and educational resources to rise up from poverty. *Webster's New World College Dictionary* defines "impoverish" as "to make poor: reduce to poverty; to deprive of strength, resources."

Those who are poor often believe that their poverty is the result of the actions of others. I think that government corruption and other forces beyond their control have impoverished some people. It is not the result of any character flaw, genetic trait, or historical legacy. Some of the poor persevere, work hard, make sacrifices, become educated, save money, and use their imaginations.

Because of their low productivity, employers cannot justify paying some individuals anything above the minimum wage. There are poor individuals who prefer leisure to work and choose to survive on welfare or charity. They miss the chance to rise up from poverty.

THE CURE FOR POVERTY

The good news is that poverty is not permanent. The poor can change their status. The benevolent rich, concerned that the gap between them and the poor could exacerbate social tensions, look for ways to avoid the tension. They fund scholarships for college and graduate school. They contribute to charities that provide for the needs of the poor.

Capital accumulation is the only way in which wages and the standard of living can increase for salaried workers. The poor benefit when the wealthy can invest capital in businesses that provide employment. The poor are then able to acquire the capital needed to compete against established businesses. In a small way, this happens all over the world; however, billions remain poor and unnoticed.

It is my opinion that enough money is available for everyone but that whoever wants wealth must be productive. In time and with productivity, I acquired financial independence, without oppressing anyone. I denied myself many pleasures. Eventually, I became financially independent.

I CHOOSE NEITHER

I refuse to be either a conservative or a liberal. The two-party system has perpetuated corruption in government, created a huge national debt, squandered our financial and natural resources, and perpetuated the class system that has caused so much poverty in this country. In short, it has brought about the demise of American democracy.

A generous god, righteous living, and benevolent people are the resources that have always been available for everyone. Many compassionate individuals offered me opportunities along the way. They championed my cause and recognized that I would be trustworthy. The same resources are available to everyone.

OUR RESPONSIBILITY

We are not born Democrats or Republicans. Our relatives, coworkers, and other factors in our spheres of influence (including television advertising) teach us to vote for the political ideologies we endorse. As adults, we must make independent and conscientious decisions for ourselves.

8

Justice

Injustice is like heart disease—a silent killer. Those who refrain from violence are sometimes the victims of vicious attacks. Those whom we would least suspect—loved ones, partners, teachers, clergymen, and so on—are often the ones who carry out unjust acts that injure us. Injustice is born of self-centeredness, deceit, hatred, and the lack of desire to do what is right. To quote Isaiah 59:15, "Truth is lacking, and he who departs from evil makes himself a prey. The Lord saw it, and it displeased him that there was no justice."

Webster's New World College Dictionary defines "justice" as:

1. The quality of being righteous; rectitude
2. Impartiality; fairness
3. The quality of being right or correct
4. Sound reason; rightfulness—validity
5. Reward or penalty as deserved; just deserts
6. The use of authority or power to uphold what is right, just or lawful.

Justice deals with what a person is due. It is our moral duty to be impartial and fair-minded in all our relationships.

TYPES OF JUSTICE

Justice has several subtypes. *Criminal* justice is lawful and fair punishment of those who commit crimes. *Distributive* justice emphasizes the idea of fair allocation and distribution of the benefits and burdens of life, including power. *Administrative* justice promotes equal treatment in the legal system.

Similarly, there are several types of injustice.

Types of Injustice

Social Injustice

A righteous society does not treat its citizens prejudicially or unjustly. However, it takes great courage to stand up for justice in a society that tolerates and even rewards prejudicial behavior. For example, because of our government's ignoring the entrance of illegal immigrants into the United States from Mexico, millions of them have worked and paid taxes here for many years. Justice dictates that they are allowed to remain and work in this country. After a stated period of time, they should be granted amnesty and citizenship, on condition that they have not violated any laws. Some lawmakers and voters are not willing to grant them amnesty or priority for citizenship. Such treatment would be unjust, and voters must let their voices be heard in Congress.

As mentioned elsewhere, the Japanese-American internment during World War II was unlawful and unjust, but the U.S. Supreme Court authorized it, and few, if any, citizens opposed it.

Political Injustice

Injustice occurs when the United States Supreme Court expands the meaning of the Constitution. Because of judicial legislation, a substantial number of people have lost the rights they had, or acquired rights they did not have, on the signing of the Constitution.

For example, the Constitution does not address the right to an abortion or mention sodomy. The Supreme Court has political reasons for its decisions on these and similar issues. But if the court creates new laws or strikes down existing laws without basing its decisions on a strict and unbiased interpretation of the Constitution, exercising such power is equivalent to declaring the Supreme Court the ultimate ruler of the United States.

Abraham Lincoln made unrelenting criticism of the court's disreputable 1857 Dred Scott decision, which held that black slaves were not citizens and therefore had no rights under the Constitution.

Franklin Roosevelt, in 1937, alleged that the Supreme Court read into the Constitution words and ideas that were not there. He solved the problem by remaking the court and appointing seven new justices between 1937 and 1941.

In 1954, the Supreme Court struck down state-sponsored school segregation. Earl Warren's justices found support for this decision in the prevailing consensus in America that apartheid was immoral. In the following forty-six years, this decision stood through many highly controversial cases. Numerous state courts followed the Supreme Court's example of judicial legislation.

Speaking at the Woodrow Wilson Center in Washington in March 2005, Supreme Court Justice Antonin Scalia denounced the idea that the Constitution is "a living document" in which judges can find new meanings that were not intended by those who wrote it. He said, "It is a legal document. It says some things and doesn't say others."

Judge Scalia and I are like-minded. It will soon be fifty years since I learned, in a course on constitutional law, that a legal document says what it means and means what it says. Neither conservatives nor liberals should read into the Constitution anything that is not specifically stated. The strict construction of the Constitution is mandatory so that no citizen will be deprived of rights granted and no citizen will have rights that were not granted. A liberal construction would cause harm to the citizens and damage to the rule of law.

Corporate Injustice

In a letter to George Logan on November 12, 1816, Thomas Jefferson, the third U.S. president (1801–1809), wrote, "I hope we shall take warning from the example and crush in it's [sic] birth the aristocracy of our moneyed corporations which dare already to challenge our government to a trial of strength and bid defiance to the laws of our country."[1]

Abraham Lincoln expressed the same concern in a letter he wrote to Col. William F. Elkins on November 21, 1864: "I see in the near future a crisis approaching that unnerves me and causes me to tremble for the safety of my country …. Corporations have been enthroned and an era of corruption in high places will follow, and the money of the country will endeavor to prolong its reign by working upon the prejudices of the people until all wealth is aggregated in a few hands and the Republic is destroyed. I feel at this moment more anxiety for the safety of my country than ever before, even in the midst of war."[2]

What Jefferson and Lincoln feared has happened in America. The original standard for the Constitution was to establish a government without fear of a state-sponsored violation of individual rights; however, because of the power of capitalism, the result has been that stockholders view the will of the people through their own lens.

1. Thomas Jefferson, *The Works of Thomas Jefferson* (New York and London: G. P. Putnam's Sons, 1905).
2. Archer H. Shaw, ed., *The Lincoln Encyclopedia* (New York: Macmillan, 1950).

In an interview with *American Conservative* magazine, Ralph Nader, corporate watchdog, said, "Corporations have taken over the government and turned it against its own people."[3]

Corporations are heavy-handed dictators. Using market power and public relations advertising, they direct our thoughts and desires, exerting enormous influence over us. This leaves us in a helpless position of serving their objectives: expanding their profits and exploiting the environment.

In general, big corporations are opposed to the core values of equality and community. Within the past forty years, personal injury lawyers have brought big corporations to their knees, especially in product liability cases. Despite the fact that management had knowledge of the danger to life and property, automobile manufacturers sold negligently designed vehicles and tires that injured or killed innocent consumers. In certain instances, the gas tank on the Ford Pinto exploded and caused death to the occupants.

I represented an attractive eighteen-year-old woman who was rendered a paraplegic in an auto accident. She was in the front passenger seat of a two-door vehicle with her seatbelt on. When her vehicle was rear-ended, the knees of the passenger behind her struck the back of her seat with such force that her spine was severed.

The construction of the front seats was in compliance with federal standards, but the manufacturer had expert evidence that the backs of the seats were unsafe. For a small additional cost, other manufacturers had designed seats that would have prevented the injury.

Rather than attempt to settle the case, the manufacturer engaged in expensive litigation and forced the injured party to incur substantial costs. On the eve before trial, the case was settled.

I completely identified with the plaintiff's attorney as played by Gene Hackman in the movie *Class Action*. In response to a subpoena for documents, the defendant, an automobile manufacturer, delivered a moving van filled with documents, in the hope that the opposing counsel would not be able to review them in less than six months. I experienced a similar treatment in my case. The defendant refused to produce, in the United States, the individual who designed the seats. After I served a subpoena for the deposition at the U.S. embassy abroad, the witness was produced in the United States.

---

3.   "Ralph Nader: Conservatively Speaking," *The American Conservative*, internet edition, June 21, 2004, http://www.amconmag.com/2004_06_21/cover.html.

Big corporations are largely self-insured and have the financial means to grind a claimant into the dust. Large insurance companies employed the same tactics prior to the enactment of laws that required them to deal in good faith with claimants.

Many major corporations were liable for punitive damages because they had knowledge of the serious injuries that their products would cause; the smoking-gun evidence was found in the corporate records. In the interest of justice and survival, we have a duty to confront the corporate plague instead of bowing to their manipulation.

Legal Injustice

The legal system in this country is out of control. Rampant fraud, abuse, and expensive lawsuits for intangible damages play havoc with our judicial system. Sometimes contingency fees cause some attorneys to exaggerate claims.

In fairness to the plaintiff bar, there are attorneys who truthfully and honestly represent plaintiffs in all kinds of injury and property damage claims against negligent corporations, reckless cigarette companies, and government defendants. They obtain large verdicts for their clients and huge fees for services; however, they advance heavy costs and a great deal of time and talent. After large verdicts, some attorneys establish foundations for the cure of diseases, for the education of children, and for other social welfare.

Many insurance companies waffle between paying millions for defense and settling exaggerated claims for much more than the expense of litigation.

Consumers pay these inflated insurance costs. A California study estimated that forty cents of every dollar paid for premiums to cover bodily injury liability and uninsured-motorist protection goes to lawyers.[4]

People in the legal profession frequently refer to civil trials as a dog-and-pony show. A civil trial is a lot like a three-ring circus, with the plaintiff's attorney playing the role of the ringmaster, entertaining and charming the jury. He hires forensic psychiatrists to sit in the courtroom and analyze each juror to determine which ones might be unfavorable to the plaintiff.

The "ringmaster" delivers a carefully scripted and memorized opening statement that exaggerates the nature and extent of his client's injuries and damages while portraying the defendant in the worst possible light. By law, he does not

---

4.   "Automobile Claims: A Study of Closed Claim Payment Patterns in California," study by the California Department of Insurance, (August 1990).

need to disclose any facts of which he is aware if the defense attorney did not admit them into evidence.

Witnesses are willing participants in this costly charade, because the dog-and-pony show mesmerizes them. The extent of witnesses' fabrications of testimony amazes me. Attorneys instruct witnesses to dress for the jury and testify to facts that are favorable to their side. Nevertheless, witnesses can have a selective memory. They "do not remember" facts that could be damaging to the party that has chosen them.

Jurors easily fall prey to the art of persuasion. Although the judge admonishes jurors to base their verdicts on the evidence, their verdicts reflect their emotions and biases.

Judges will tell jurors that no insurance company is a party to the litigation and they should not consider insurance in their deliberations. What jurors usually do not know is that the money to pay the claims for injuries and property damage eventually comes out of the pockets of the public, in the form of increased premiums charged by the insurance companies.

Because of expensive medical malpractice verdicts, insurance premiums increased to such an extreme that many surgeons stopped performing surgery; some allowed their malpractice insurance to lapse (while continuing to perform surgery); and numerous older doctors retired early. As with many of my statements, they are based on my reasonable investigation, observations, and discussions with the parties involved. In some instances, my efforts to document them with evidence were not productive. I am not writing a professional journal, but I tell it as I see it, and I expect readers to disbelieve the statements or make their own investigations.

Religious Injustice

One would expect that injustice would stop at the door of God's representatives. History proves otherwise. Religion has served as reason to murder, to segregate, to wage war, and to commit to all manner of crimes against humanity.

In the Crusades, the Inquisition, and the witch hunts, religion was a mirror image of the mob mentality. The purpose of the Crusades, for example, was to take Jerusalem back from the "infidels" (Muslims). These "infidels" defeated the Crusaders in the final battle. Muslims still harbor hatred for the Western countries because of the Crusades.

People in the free world do not understand how law-abiding Germans could abandon their principles and embrace Hitler. As I reflect on the events that led to the Nazi regime, I recognize several possible motives for this conduct. Some people did not want to agitate those in power. Others were foolish enough to believe that the conduct was harmless. Still others did not realize that they were practicing deceit.

In the Nazi regime, the Crusades, the Inquisition, and the witch hunts, religious and political extremists believed that they alone knew the truth. In each of these ideologies, the leaders desired to eliminate those who did not agree with them.

A PARABLE OF JUSTICE

Plato's *Republic* includes a dialogue between Glaucon and Socrates on the origin of justice.[5] According to Glaucon, it is more advantageous to perform an unjust act (as long as one is not punished for it) than to suffer injustice without the power of revenge. Acting with injustice is less evil than being the victim of it. When men are unable to avoid injustice, they try to create laws against it. Unjust men would have to be out of their minds to enact such laws that were contrary to their interest; nevertheless, they did.

Glaucon continued his dialogue with Socrates by telling a story about a shepherd named Gyges, who found a ring that made him invisible when he turned it around on his finger. Gyges used his newfound ability to seduce the queen and take over the kingdom.

Most readers of this story would say the shepherd behaved improperly. They would praise a person who refrained from becoming invisible in order to do wrong. Privately, though, they would see a person of such noble character as an idiot. Few men would refrain from taking the property of another if assured they could do so safely and without reprisal.

Taking the property of another is the darkness (evil urge) that is in each one of us. God created the evil urge in his plan for salvation. Glaucon had a valid point, and I agree with his conclusion.

Glaucon argued that the just man is the best of men, yet he is usually thought to be the worst. When the just man and the unjust man reach the outermost extreme, Glaucon opines that the unjust man is the happier of the two. Many Americans would agree with him on this point. I say that the unjust man is dumb but as happy as the revelers in Times Square on New Year's Eve.

---

5.   Plato, The Republic, Book II, written in 360 BC, trans. Benjamin Jowett (New York: C. Scribner's Sons, 1871).

Because the devil encourages his followers and helps them to prosper, unjust men seem to have power, favor, honor, possessions, and every comfort.

MOTIVES FOR JUSTICE

David Hume (1711–1776), noted historian and essayist, indicated that benevolence and regard for public interest are not the original motives for justice. The imperfect justice we see around us restricts us from concluding anything about justice in the universe. Nature made inadequate provision for men's wants, and justice derives its origin from the selfishness and confined generosity of men.[6]

Contrary to Hume's belief, I think that selfishness and confined generosity of men might not be the original motives for justice. I embrace the virtue of justice on the belief in a just and moral God and not on human convention. In my opinion, his proposition that man's impressions are not natural to the mind of man is erroneous. It is natural to my mind and perhaps to other minds.

OUR RESPONSIBILITY

> *He has showed you, O man, what is good; and what does the LORD require of you but to do justice, and to love kindness, and to walk humbly with your God?*

> Micah 6:8

Hopefully, you have learned from this chapter that it takes great courage to stand up for justice in an America that tolerates and even rewards prejudicial behavior. What Jefferson and Lincoln feared has come to pass. An era of corporate corruption is upon us. The money of the country has prolonged the corporations' reign by working upon the prejudices of the people, and all wealth has been aggregated in a few hands. As a consequence, the republic has declined.

---

6.   David Hume, *A Treatise of Human Nature: Being an Attempt to Introduce the Experimental Method of Reasoning into Moral Subjects*, Book III "Of Morals," Part II "Of Justice and Injustice," sec. ii "Of the Origin of Justice and Property," (1739–1740).

Unless the LORD builds the house, those who build it labor in vain. Unless the LORD watches over the city, the watchman stays awake in vain.

Psalms 127:1

This book was meant for readers who do not know and believe this truth. The skeptics scoff at the word of God—the Bible. But there comes a time when a skeptic ought to examine the foundation on which he builds his life. Is there anything that I have disclosed that convinces you to explore God incarnate in Jesus Christ? If so, you hunger for more than any human can give you; therefore, seriously consider pursuing this truth.

9

Political Correctness

Several years ago, my wife and I attended an informal church dinner at the home of one of the members. The senior minister and I sat at the same table. In our brief conversation, he maintained that the truth does not depend upon the character of the teacher. In my opinion, this statement is misleading.

I told him that ministers have a serious obligation not to contradict what they say by what they do. I have no doubt that I, a sinner, have the capacity to declare that Jesus is the embodiment of truth and inspires truth; nevertheless, I have a serious obligation not to contradict what I affirm by what I do. Here, the emphasis is on obligation and not on the capacity of a sinner to speak the truth. In other words, what you do confirms what you teach. If you declare that Jesus is lord, then you have a serious obligation not to contradict his commandments. We did not pursue the discussion. In my experience, clergymen generally do not welcome the opinions of nonprofessionals.

I happened to know that the associate minister in his church had committed adultery and was deprived of the rank or function of a minister (defrocked). Adultery committed by ministers in his denomination had become such a problem that it required a rehabilitation program.

Many Christian organizations and popular evangelists have been the subjects of well-publicized cases of financial and sexual exploitation of believers. Jimmy Swaggart, Jim Bakker, and Ted Haggard are recent examples of fundamentalist ministers who committed adultery and were defrocked. Haggard, a Colorado Springs minister with a congregation of fourteen thousand people, was taking drugs and having sex with a male prostitute. It is no wonder people outside the Church view Christians with suspicion. All mortals are flawed in some capacity; however, many mortals know right from wrong, do not yield to Satan's temptations, and, by the power of the holy spirit, run from the temptation to take drugs and have illicit sex. I believe that a person who has a corrupted character is a bad example, is untrustworthy, and should not teach. I am not speaking about his or her capacity to declare the truth; I am talking about accountability.

The hostess of the church dinner later told my wife that my outspoken disagreement with her invited guest was humiliating, and I was not to darken the door of her house again. When my wife told me this, I experienced the freedom of being politically incorrect.

For the purpose of this discussion, I define "politically correct" as any conduct or statement that leads others to believe that the speaker might not question the voice of the people or those in power, when in fact he does. For example, party members do not often speak ill of other party members, and they often are inclined to ignore the criminal and immoral conduct of fellow members. They often overlook violations of the rule of law and pardon the culprits.

The desire to be politically correct controls many aspects of American life. Spouses sacrifice truth to maintain peace in the household. Children tell their parents what they know the parents want to hear. Employees strive to be politically correct in order to appease their employers.

Religious and educational institutions, diplomats, governments, countries, civilizations, and scores of others tell little white lies to avoid offending others, especially those in positions of authority. In its simplest terms, being politically correct requires deceit.

According to the French philosopher Jean-Jacques Rousseau, "Man is born free but everywhere is in chains."[1] He was referring to social and political inequality. I take the liberty of expanding the meaning of "chains" to include any submissive conduct or statement made in the name of political correctness.

Most of Americans' misfortunes come from having too high an opinion of public officials, religious leaders, educators, celebrities, and so forth. Many of them are not worthy of the honor we bestow upon them. We enhance their cause when we lead others to believe that we do not question their conduct and statements.

Kowtowing is an old Chinese custom of touching the ground with the forehead as a sign of submission. In ancient Greece, some citizens chose to bow instead of questioning the state. A brave few challenge wrongdoers and risk the consequences. For example, Cindy Sheehan challenged Bush on the war in Iraq and called the Bush administration "reckless" and "insane" "maniacs" running America. She warned Senator Clinton, "End your support for the war in Iraq, or

---

1.   "Discourse on Inequality," from Jean-Jacques Rousseau, *The Social Contract and Discourses*, translated by.G. D. H. Cole (London: J.M. Dent, 1913), pages 207–238.

else." In May 2007, she quit the Democratic Party over their support for the Iraq funding bill.

Political correctness cheapens honesty and squelches our search for truth. Criticism is essential for testing our fundamental beliefs, convictions, and values. In order to have an intelligible world, we must adopt a critical perspective about the prevailing political, corporate, educational, social, religious, and other views offered as "truth." We even need to challenge our own deceitful hearts.

Political correctness is foolish appeasement, and I cannot understand how any spiritual individual can justify such deception in any circumstance.

OUR RESPONSIBILITY

Be courageous and honest. If you are politically correct, as defined in this chapter, you cannot be honest to yourself and others. Start on a small scale, by speaking out when you have valid reasons to disagree with friends, family, clergymen, professors, government, political parties, or other individuals or institutions. Be prepared to offer alternatives that are beneficial to others and yourself. Be committed to truth in all circumstances, and know that there are no substitutes. Be willing to stake your life on truth and love.

10

Freedom

Americans today proclaim how much they value their freedom. We have the right to cast a ballot. We can travel between states and to foreign lands. We have the right to speak. We can say whatever we want about anybody, as long as we do not slander or libel him or her. But our freedom is substantially restricted by an overwhelming number of known and unknown, real and imaginary antagonists that relentlessly affect our daily lives.

SIN

In the beginning, God gave Adam and Eve the choice to obey or disobey him. Unfortunately for them and for all their descendants, the first human beings chose disobedience. As a result, we have relationship difficulties, endless struggles to survive, and "dust in the wind" mortality.

> *Then the Lord God said, "Behold, the man has become like one of us, knowing good and evil; and now, lest he put forth his hand and take also of the tree of life, and eat, and live for ever ..."*

Genesis 3:22

> *In the sweat of your face you shall eat bread till you return to the ground, for out of it you were taken; you are dust, and to dust you shall return.*

Genesis 3:19

We may shake our heads at Adam and Eve's decision, which had such far-reaching effects down through the ages. But the truth is that each of us sins, in one way or another.

Slothfulness

Since I am not inclined to be lazy, I sometimes become irritated with people who "thank God it's Friday." My irritation rises to a state of anger when others expect me to pay the price for their neglect or irresponsibility. I have deprived myself of many personal needs in order to provide for others who were too lazy and irresponsible to provide for themselves. For example, I need love; time to myself; the excitement of preparing for and successfully completing a remarkable jury trial; the rare, quiet serenity in nature, contemplating the majesty of the creator; inspiration I receive listening to classical music, especially opera; the company of friends with enough common sense to understand my remarks; and harmony in a self-centered world filled with discord. I do not need someone to take care of me, and I do not need to be needed all the time. For the past forty-six years, I have not had enough time to attend to these needs.

In Proverbs 24:30–32, King Solomon received instructions by observing a field owned by a lazy person. I received instruction from Solomon's wisdom; unlike Solomon, I become irritated with the excessive number of lazy people who idle away their time during the work week. They are bored and lethargic at work, enthusiastic and energetic at play.

> *I passed by the field of a sluggard, by the vineyard of a man without sense; and lo, it was all overgrown with thorns; the ground was covered with nettles, and its stone wall was broken down. Then I saw and considered it; I looked and received instruction.*

Proverbs 24:30–32

Obviously, the sluggard was foolish and dimwitted. He did not want to receive instructions, because he believed he knew enough already; nevertheless, he had no capacity to understand and was unable to make use of his property.

The sluggard remains idle in the hope that God will assume responsibility for his well-being. He has no purpose, and he wastes valuable time. He has opportunities that he does not use, obligations that he does not fulfill, and capacities that he does not exercise.

If one does not farm a field for God, the soul will yield its natural produce. What is the natural produce of your children if you leave them untrained for God?

If we are slothful, the natural produce of our hearts will be most inconvenient and unpleasant. Nobody can sleep on thorns or make a pillow of nettles. No rest can come out of idleness.

While you are sleeping, Satan will be sowing. If you withhold the seed of good, Satan will be lavish with the seed of evil, and from that evil will come anguish and regret. Neglect produces evil.

Individuals can sow the seed of good in these ways:

Physical Works of Mercy

- Feed the hungry

- Give drink to the thirsty

- Clothe the naked

- Shelter the homeless

- Comfort the imprisoned

- Visit the sick

- Bury the dead

Spiritual Works of Mercy

- Admonish sinners

- Instruct the uninformed

- Counsel the doubtful

- Comfort the sorrowful

- Be patient with those in error

- Forgive offenses

- Pray for the living and the dead

Anger

Anger, also called wrath, manifests itself in the individual who sets aside reason for fury. You can expect misery and despair from being angry without just cause; however, there is a time and a place for anger.

Righteous Anger

God himself gets angry when he sees unrighteous behavior and evil. A just god demands repentance. Both the Old and New Testaments record that God and Jesus were angry about evil. We, his children, made in his image, cannot witness immorality without similar feelings of anger. We should be angry about wrong-doing, for our own sakes and for that of others.

Responses to Anger

Everyone needs divine wisdom to know how to respond appropriately to anger. If your anger is selfish or unjustified, you need to learn how to deal with that emotion and let it go without harming yourself or others. A mysterious freedom comes from the willing withdrawal from an argument with your adversaries.

When you experience righteous anger, pray that God will give you the courage to uphold justice, promote peace, and love those who antagonize you. St. Paul in Ephesians 4:26–27 condones anger but not revenge. In addition, he admonishes us not to stay angry. Those who repress anger can be certain that it will fester inside and eventually manifest itself in revenge. Naïve individuals look with disdain on people who get angry, but they are unaware that their conduct provokes the anger. St. Paul does not give license to individuals to make a habit of anger. In Ephesians 4:26–27, he says, "Go ahead and be angry. You do well to be angry—but do not use your anger as fuel for revenge. In addition, do not stay angry. Do not go to bed angry."

OUR RESPONSE TO THE ENEMIES OF OUR FREEDOM

Jesus said, "Love your enemies and pray for those who persecute you" (Matthew 5:44). This is difficult to do, but God is our helper. As best we can, we need to be faithful, even in the face of madness and evil.

I pray that God will forgive my enemies so they will accept Christ as their savior. After all, before I made a commitment to Christ, I was in the same condition as they are now.

THE SLAVERY OF COMMITMENT

About thirty years ago, I heard a quiet voice within me cry, "I want to be free." I yearned to be free from the bondage of pursuing the American dream. I did not want to spend my life fulfilling the desires of other people, yet I was a slave to my job and to unwise commitments I had made. I felt lonely, empty, unhappy, and irritable.

One of the sad realities of our culture is that too many people are simply irresponsible. With few exceptions, I did the work myself if I wanted something done right. My plea to others to share responsibility produced hostility. Seeing no honorable alternative, I continued to protect others from adverse consequences. I suffered repeated burnout and endless fatigue while honoring my commitments. My failure to confront the lies only perpetuated wickedness. When I sanctioned manipulation, evil prevailed.

Commitments are necessary in all relationships; however, indiscriminate and sentimental commitments can be detrimental to one's physical, mental, and spiritual well-being. Almost all relationships and commitments enslave us to some degree. They consume our time and energy in one way or another. But it can be difficult to say no to manipulative individuals or oppressive institutions.

Often, by the time we become aware of a consuming relationship or commitment, it is too late to back out without undue hardship on all sides. At some point, though, it is imperative that we break out of this prison and reclaim our lives.

QUIET DESPERATION

It is incongruous that an evangelical Christian can be a conscious participant in causing such quiet desperation in the life of another, yet it happens far more often than we would imagine. For example, prejudice and hate take many forms, and often those involved are unconscious of their conduct. The victims live in quiet desperation because of the color of their skin, their natural origins, their religion, or their socioeconomic class. It is shameless hypocrisy when self-righteous groups ship food, clothing, and funds to people in other lands but refuse to seek them out in the community where they live.

Equally as blatant is the situation in which family members live in a household where one or more members selfishly manipulate, oppress, and abuse a victim or victims. The injured person is generally submissive, but not always. Even an assertive individual can be manipulated by a self-centered, capricious individual.

Henry David Thoreau once wrote, "The mass of men lead lives of quiet desperation. What is called resignation is confirmed desperation."[1] The quietly desperate person usually goes unnoticed and is taken for granted.

TRUE FREEDOM

Authentic freedom demands complete surrender to divine will. We have devoted ourselves to the commitments that our American culture claims are worthy and honorable, and they are not always congruent with a complete surrender to God.

For instance, today we are committed to a war in Iraq that President Bush claims is America's responsibility to fight, for the cause of freedom in the Middle East. There is now a civil war in Iraq, and tens of thousands of innocent men, women, and children have been killed. Several thousand American servicemen have been killed or permanently injured, and it is forecast that we will remain in Iraq for at least another eighteen months. The money spent on this war would have been better used to improve the quality of life for impoverished Americans.

In my opinion, the Iraq war is unconscionable. The parents of servicemen killed in Iraq are numb with grief and disbelief, yet some of our leaders pretend to honor the servicemen who died for their country. I grieve that they have died in vain.

There are other commitments that our culture claims are worthy and honorable and that I think are incongruent with a complete surrender to God. I have a great deal more to say about them in subsequent chapters.

Conscientiously and in good faith, I asked God's guidance and entered into life-altering commitments and relationships. With hindsight, I learned that my decisions were hasty and based on erroneous assumptions. I concluded that I was totally responsible for the human error and that God was in no way responsible.

I studied the philosophical and theological arguments for and against divine providence and free will for fifty years or more, and I will share with you my

---

1.   Henry David Thoreau, *Walden*, (Boston: Ticknor & Fields 1854).

present thoughts on the subject. St. Augustine concluded that providence will remain more or less a mystery. Catholic dogma regards eternal happiness primarily as the work of God and his grace, but secondarily as the fruit and reward of the meritorious actions of the believer.

A clergyman gazed upon a fertile field of crops and remarked to the owner, "God has abundantly blessed you with this crop."

The farmer responded, "I pray and I pray as though everything depends on God, and I work and I work as though everything depends on me." The crop could have been destroyed by natural causes, erroneously referred to as an "act of God."

OUR RESPONSIBILITY

We are incapable of fully understanding the depth of God's love. This being true, we cannot love God, our neighbors, or ourselves as we truly ought to. Until we see God face to face, we may not love wisely; however, we should strive to love others as our merciful lord loves us.

We often abandon truth in an erroneous notion of sacrificial love. We turn the other check and allow antagonists to prosper. We accede to a pouter's insistences, and the world becomes wicked.

Truth will not triumph if we are not courageous enough to say, as Martin Luther did, "Having been conquered by the Scriptures ... and my conscience taken captive by the word of God, I cannot and will not revoke anything, for it is neither safe nor right to act against one's conscience. God help me. Amen."[2]

---

2.   Arthur Cushman McGiffert, *Martin Luther, the Man and His Work* (New York: The Century, 1911), p. 203.

11

A Man's Home Is His Castle

A man's home is his castle. This saying is as old as the basic concepts of English common law. English jurist Sir Edward Coke (1552–1634) wrote, *"Et domus, sua cuique tutissimum refugium"* ("One's home is the safest refuge for all"). Nevertheless, in America, our homes are no longer a refuge. This country does not belong to us, its inhabitants, anymore. On the contrary, political leaders with personal agendas usurp control of the home without permission of the owners.

CHAOS IN THE CASTLE

A Man's Family, His Castle?

A benefactor sometimes sacrifices to provide the beneficiary with a life of luxury. The unfortunate result is often that the beneficiary loses his incentive to work. He and his ne'er-do-well companions end up condemning the benefactor as a money-grubbing capitalist.

When I first came to San Francisco, I lived at 864 Ashbury Street in the Haight-Ashbury district. There were many restored Victorian homes in my neighborhood. Haight Street was lined with all kinds of clothing and food stores, laundromats, restaurants, and so on. This district bordered Golden Gate Park. In the sixties, during the Vietnam War, young adults opposed to the war camped in the park and strolled along Haight Street. Locals and tourists visited the area to watch the flower children demonstrate against the war. In a short period of time, the clothing stores were under new management and selling used clothes. The restaurants provided a menu in keeping with the taste of the new neighborhood. Thus the new era in the district was born, and it became known as the "hippie era." Simultaneously, there were demonstrations at the universities in the San Francisco Bay Area.

Some of the young adults hanging out in Haight-Ashbury were offspring of prominent people in the Bay Area. The children of a friend, the managing partner of an old and prestigious law firm, condemned their old dad for representing a major oil company in order to earn their daily bread. At the same time, they lived in a luxurious house, attended notable universities, and traveled the world at Dad's expense. Some preached the "good news" of free love and wore flowers in their hair or turkey feathers behind their ears. Their motto, "Make love, not war," was a way to berate their parents for engaging in a capitalist system and supporting the war. Some parents had feelings of dishonor, unworthiness, and embarrassment because of their children's rebellion and lifestyles—quite a high price to pay for their unselfish benevolence.

Nowadays in many households, both parents work outside the home in order to meet the cost of living and save for future necessities; therefore, both parents should have a say in the management of the household.

Unfortunately, many American families today are financially irresponsible. The average household has insufficient savings for future needs, yet most families have plenty of funds to spend on unnecessary stuff that is soon discarded.

I am dumbfounded whenever I see the amount of money low-income families spend for souvenirs and food at amusement parks and other entertainment venues. The cause of this madness is not as obvious as it seems. They have nothing to fill the inner void they feel.

Most Americans do not know what is causing their inner yearning. Then again, I do not believe it would make a difference if they knew.

The Dysfunctional Family

In recent years, we have heard a great deal about the dysfunctional family in America. In my opinion, families become dysfunctional when stubborn and undisciplined members receive unearned privileges, then demand entitlements. Fully financed college education, world travel, chauffeured transportation, financial aid, and future inheritance are some of these unearned yet expected privileges.

Also, I believe chaos and dysfunction result whenever any member of the family usurps the authority of the head of the house. For the sake of order, children should make their requests known to the parents; however, the parents should have the final decision, and children should not question their authority.

Families Bond through Struggle

When a family is in "survival mode," it tends to function as a single unit. People who are not in survival mode usually focus on selfish desires of the flesh. In an affluent society, most upper-income families seek instant gratification. When they prosper, they provide their family with many privileges. As a result, they end up becoming slaves to their work and commitments.

In my childhood family, the desire to survive bonded us. My father and mother worked from sunup until sundown to support our family. At an early age, my two brothers and I witnessed the great effort and angst of our parents. We were mindful that they went through hard times to provide us with necessities, and we wanted to be a part of the struggle to earn a living.

I concealed injuries from my parents in an effort to spare them grief. The summer before my sophomore year in college, I was driving my older brother's Ford sedan, with no tread on the tires, to a coal-mining town to sell produce. When returning home, the car skidded on wet pavement, and my head went through the windshield. The car was a total loss. In addition, I was unsuccessful in hiding my injuries.

Following a brief case of hysteria, my mother survived the emotional trauma. My father borrowed money from a relative to pay for my medical expenses. I returned to college to finish my sophomore year, and I paid the tuition and living expenses by working odd jobs.

Some families do not realize that the head of a household has exposure to grueling conditions and circumstances in order to ensure the family's survival. Consequently, the breadwinner feels alone, unloved, unhappy, and angry. When he mentions the cause of his despair, the children blame him for the disharmony in the family and relegate him to the role of a villain.

A MAN'S JOB, HIS CASTLE?

Most people in this country long for a high standard of living and all the comforts that affluence provides. In an effort to achieve this coveted state, the head of the household pays for the mortgage, private education, medical and life insurance, weddings, vacations, vehicles, and retirement benefits. If anything is left, he may create trusts for the education of the grandchildren and a nest egg for the surviving spouse and children. That is, after all, what many affluent heads of households call success.

However, the Internal Revenue Service and the state franchise tax boards effectively deprive refuge to the lord of the castle. As agents of the government, they rob the country's hard-working and responsible citizens of half of their gross income in order to provide for the overcompensated members of Congress, to give aid to foreign countries, to pay for military defense, and to provide entitlements to special groups.

A MAN'S COUNTRY, HIS CASTLE?

Fierce debates occurred over the form of government that would be agreeable to all of the original thirteen colonies. A strong federal government and a confederation of states were the two choices.

Although we have a federal government that has power over the states, the states have specific rights to govern themselves. States have separate constitutions, but their constitutions cannot be in conflict with the federal constitution. The conflict between states' rights and federal supremacy still exists.

The demographics of each state have changed beyond the capability of the present Constitution to be the law of the land. The founders of this nation, who drafted the Constitution, had no way to foresee the country's future growth, problems, demographics, racial prejudices, political ideologies, religious belief and unbelief, slavery, civil war, world wars, and same-sex marriage. Our ancestors did not draft the Constitution for present-day Americans.

It is my belief that the founders would draft a new constitution today instead of allowing the Supreme Court to interpret its meaning.

A MAN'S CHURCH, HIS CASTLE?

Having lost faith in my country, I sought refuge in a local church. The only time the reverend made a call at my house was when he had a favor to ask. I was one of the affluent members of the congregation, so he asked me to pledge a large contribution to the capital improvement program. After making my pledge, I discovered that the reverend believed that the Bible was wrong about homosexuality. I disagreed with the reverend's opinion and transferred my church membership.

Liberal theology is another reason for the ungodliness in America. Liberal ministers and seminaries confuse Christian love with acceptance of another's lifestyle that is contrary to conscience and to God's word. They believe that love means condoning sin; however, this kind of across-the-board acceptance is not a principle taught in the scriptures.

APPROPRIATE PARALLELS

A refuge is a fantasy in the sky. Now you see it, and now you do not. In a sense, a castle represents carnality, and faith is the assurance of things hoped for, the conviction of things not seen.

Fyodor Dostoevsky, the great nineteenth-century Russian writer, included a parable in the "Grand Inquisitor" chapter of his novel *The Brothers Karamazov*. In this story, Jesus returns to earth during the Spanish Inquisition. The cardinal of Seville interrogates Christ in his cell. Dostoevsky, using the cardinal as his proxy, argues that people value authority and material comfort over faith.

> In the end, they will lay their freedom at our feet, and say to us, "Make us your slaves, but feed us." … And men rejoiced that they were again led like sheep, and that the terrible gift (freedom) that had brought them such suffering was, at last, lifted from their hearts.[1]

Suppose Jesus came to America today in the same manner he did in *The Brothers Karamazov*. He would be an embarrassment to those who pursue political agendas in his name. He would not be an asset to the special-interest groups that use him to justify their goals. Christ left no example or command for the Church to arrogate political power for itself. What could those who seek that power say to him if he returned, except: "Why have you come to hinder us?"

OUR RESPONSIBILITY

The righteous in America need to be aware that neither they nor our country are everlasting. It is futile to struggle against the inevitable fall of the American empire. Along the way, we can bring good tidings to the afflicted, comfort the

---

1. Fyodor Dostoyevsky, *The Brothers Karamazov*, Unabridged, trans. Constance Garnett, ed. Manuel Komroff, 1957 (New York: Signet Classic/New American Library–1989). (N.B: The book was originally published in 1881, a year before Dostoyevsky's death).

brokenhearted, proclaim liberty to the captives, and open the prisons of those who are bound (see Isaiah 61:1).

12

Ambition

Ambition is universal, and it is at the core of many great works. At the same time, ambition is the foundation of the prosperity of the wicked and the class system. Ambition, like the evil urge, can lead people astray. Ambition serves us, and if we ignore it within us, it will remain as uncontrolled passion, without direction.

In Shakespeare's play *Julius Caesar*, Caesar, having recognized his friend Brutus among the assassins, utters three famous words: "Et tu, Brute?" ("And you, Brutus?") We still use this phrase today to express surprise and dismay at the treachery of a supposed friend.

Yet in Marc Anthony's funeral speech over Caesar, whom Brutus has helped to kill, Anthony calls Brutus an honorable and noble man.

> The evil that men do lives after them; the good is oft interrèd with their bones. So let it be with Caesar … He was my friend, faithful and just to me. But Brutus says he was ambitious, and Brutus is an honorable man … When that the poor have cried, Caesar hath wept. Ambition should be made of sterner stuff.[1]

This description of Brutus as noble and honorable is intentionally facetious. Using irony, Marc Anthony is actually attempting to portray this killer as ungrateful and treacherous. His speech succeeds in turning the Roman people against Brutus and his fellow assassins.

Shakespeare seems to be saying here that Brutus's treacherous betrayal was not as significant as his false accusation that Caesar was ambitious.

---

1.   William Shakespeare, Julius Caesar, Act 3, Scene 2, (c.f., http://www.shakespeare-literature.com/).

NEGATIVE AMBITION

If I consent to God's presence in all of my business and personal affairs, he will be involved in my life. If I build with pride, vanity, oppression, and injustice, God will not participate in my affairs. If I do not acknowledge God, I have no reason to expect his blessing, and without his blessing, all is nothing. My best-laid plans will fail unless God honors them with success. If I depend upon my own contrivance, I labor in vain.

What is it that we are supposed to build? The very question assumes that we are obligated to build for someone else's purposes. It behooves us to know whether we are building for ourselves, parents, family, government, corporations, or God.

POSITIVE AMBITION

Ambition is not always a negative trait. *Webster's New World College Dictionary* defines "ambition" as "a strong desire to gain a particular objective; specific, the drive to succeed, or to gain fame, power, wealth, etc." Such strong desires can be for good or for evil.

In Shakespeare's *Henry VIII*, Cardinal Wolsey says to Cromwell, "I charge thee, fling away ambition; by that sin fell the angels."[2] Following Wolsey's advice would accomplish nothing. Ambition is necessary for men to do great deeds. We need a strong desire to gain a godly objective.

I have yet to meet a person who is ambitious about loving God and his neighbor. Most people are ambitious for the things of the world, particularly fame and fortune; however, whether they realize it or not, what they are actually yearning for is God. We are created to love the lord, our god, and he expects us to love our neighbors as ourselves (see Mark 12:30–31). "So faith, hope, love abide, these three; but the greatest of these is love" (1 Corinthians 13:13).

Because numerous people in our culture are manipulative and wrongfully ambitious, I love them harshly, as I love myself. I love them in the same manner as Christ did when he drove the moneychangers out of the temple with a whip. He loved them with justice, as he loves us.

I will address this subject in detail in the chapter on self-centeredness.

---

2.   William Shakespeare, Henry VIII, Act 3, Scene 2 (c.f., http://www. shakespeare-literature.com/).

WHAT ARE YOU BUILDING?

To analyze the value of what you are building in your life, I suggest that you prepare three lists. In one, describe what you are building for yourself. In the second, list what you are doing to please God. In the third, identify why your labor has been in vain. Study these lists before you waste your life doing what you ought not to do.

I prepared these three lists when I was thirty-five years old. Through them, I discovered that I was trying to serve God and attend to my own desires at the same time, and this was an impossible task. I learned that excessive care about the things of this world is a vain and fruitless undertaking. My ambition to be successful was rooted in the fear of failure, misfortune, prejudice, and deceit that disguised itself as virtue. I did not love God with all my heart, soul, mind, and strength.

In the heading of the third list, I asked, "What happened?" I came up with approximately fifty reasons why I was not seeking to do what was pleasing to God. Several of the most important ones fell into the categories of sin, evil, ignorance, temptation, double-mindedness, fear, self-centeredness, loneliness, and selfish desires.

The American way beguiles many to have excessive care about the things of this world, yet those very things make life miserable for those enslaved to provide them. This is the ultimate betrayal.

GOOD AND BAD AMBITION

Few have the ambition to walk the path of the saints. Many more have unbridled ambition that places a stranglehold on others. In the business section of any bookstore, you will find titles such as these:

> *Swim with the Sharks without Being Eaten Alive: Outsell, Outmanage, Outmotivate, and Outnegotiate Your Competition*[3]
> *How to Sell Anything to Anybody*[4]

---

3. Harvey Mackay, Swim with the Sharks without Being Eaten Alive: Outsell, Outmanage, Outmotivate, and Outnegotiate Your Competition, (New York: Ballantine Books, 1996).
4. Joe Girard, with Stanley H. Brown, *How to Sell Anything to Anybody*, (New York: Warner Books, 1986).

The Ultimate Secret to Getting Absolutely Everything You Want[5]

These books are best-sellers because U.S. citizens desire to get their share of the American way, regardless of whom they have to betray along the way. I too once believed this lie. I used to dream about obtaining wealth, fame, and power. Alas, to what end?

Americans, with all their humanitarian goals, have accomplished many positive things. Nevertheless, most people have strong narcissistic motives for gaining fame, power, and wealth. In nearly every vocation, self-interest prevails over the interests of humankind.

Why might this be more prevalent in America than in other civilizations? There are greater opportunities to fulfill worldly ambitions in this country than elsewhere, so Americans are tempted to place personal interests above God and the common good.

In recent days, we have witnessed corporate and personal ambitions run amok. Righteous Americans are living alongside ungodly, corrupt individuals. Betrayal is all around us.

OUR RESPONSIBILITY

Things are not what they seem; therefore, a wise person will look for facts to match reality. He will consider the spiritual and physical consequences of his actions. A foolish person, on the other hand, builds on an unstable foundation, without regard to physical and spiritual perils.

Because of pride and vanity, naïve believers become gossipers and busybodies, meddling in egotistical religious activities and studies. We must be vigilant, so that we do not fall prey to Satan, the master betrayer of humanity.

The storms of life test the stability of our foundations. Foolish people build their lives on lies, deception, and betrayal. Wise people build their lives on the embodiment of truth, Jesus Christ, who cannot fail. Those who do not hear and obey the embodiment of truth are building on sand, and great will be their fall. Those who do follow Christ are building on a rock. If you trust in him, no betrayal against you will succeed.

---

5.   Michael Hernacki, The Ultimate Secret to Getting Absolutely Everything You Want, (New York: Berkley Trade, 2001).

13

Violence

American history, like all history, is largely a story of violence. Violence is a tragedy in which everyone involved is exposed to the risk of moral corruption and physical destruction.

Dr. James Gilligan, in his book *Violence: Reflections on a National Epidemic*, observes, "It is remarkable to me how seldom people recognize the extent to which many of the criminals of today are contemporary versions of our own ancestors."[1]

Most people think of violence as antisocial behavior that they do not see within themselves. Violence, wickedness, revenge, and evil are within all of us. "None is righteous, no, not one" (Romans 3:10).

THE ROOT CAUSES OF VIOLENCE

Pride

I say that many self-righteous individuals cannot accept that they have a propensity for violence; however, this attitude actually makes them susceptible to the very violence they deny. Shy, sensitive people allow others to trample on them. Overbearing people step on those who get in their way, even loved ones, often without realizing that they are doing so.

According to Dr. Gilligan, we view the violence of others critically and through a microscope and our own as insignificant. "When we denounce and condemn the wave of violence occurring today, we always mean other people's violence," he says. What we read in the newspapers about the "enemies of society" is a view of the other side, and we monopolize on the concept of good and

---

1.   Dr. James Gilligan, *Violence: Reflections on a National Epidemic* (NewYork: Vintage, 1997), p. 245.

evil. Decent, intelligent, kind people can suddenly erupt into brutal violence in words, thoughts, or deeds. They might try to reassure themselves with the thought that it was only a passing accident in the heat of the moment. They would be better off if they recognized this aspect of themselves instead of denying it.[2]

Shame and Humiliation

I know firsthand the scares inflicted on me by a class society that made it a habit to shame and humiliate me and others because of our national origin and religion. Rather than react with violence, I forgave them, because I knew the darkness in each one of us. Equally important, I worked hard to learn the truth and to develop character.

As a child, my father taught me the difference between right and wrong, good and evil. He told me about the children mentioned in the Old Testament. God was real for me, and I grew in faith and wisdom. As a sinner, I am a living example of what God will do in the life of anyone who will trust in him.

There is violence within each of us, and we need a supernatural power to unite this evil urge with the good urge. When we do this, we can fulfill God's commandments to love him and one another. It would be helpful for you to review the chapters on good and evil and love in order to make the connection between these two urges.

Lack of Self-Esteem

For years, I have seen many people in all walks of life that have been rejected or abandoned, slighted or demeaned, humiliated or ridiculed, dishonored or disrespected, and their loss is my loss. It is not possible for me to be content when there is needless suffering around me. I truly grieve over unknown souls who are slowly disintegrating before my eyes.

I am exasperated and troubled about the wicked people in high places who are responsible for the disintegration of the souls and bodies of our fellow men. My god is not only a god of love but also a god of justice. I look to the time when his wrath will rain down on all the unrighteous.

---

2.   Ibid., pp. 241–244.

Poverty

Poverty among black residents in Washington DC has resulted in an infant mortality rate of twenty-one deaths per 1,000 live births, and this rate matches third-world levels.[3]

Celebrities are swarming in Washington to induce Bush and Congress to send aid to Africa. African Americans have rallied in Washington to rouse the conscience of Congress and Americans about their plight. Civil rights bills have not remedied the condition. The media has given extensive coverage of it. Nevertheless, poverty is still around.

In a previous chapter, I gave my opinion about the causes and cures of poverty. I do more than complain; however, the work of individuals and charities is inadequate. I have no clue what God has in mind about poverty in America and throughout the world. God knows what is going on, including my venting of frustration with the wicked and my lack of peace. Since everything appears to have failed, it is time that I take a vacation, and I do not mean to go someplace. The best way for me to describe it is this: to quit trying, to quit not trying, to quit quitting. Neither the decline of America nor the human conditions are going to go away, but truth and love are left. For a while, take a vacation to experience this truth and love.

Politicians and citizens, blinded by patriotism and heritage, cause an increase in violence by shaming, dishonoring, and humiliating those who live in poverty. When I walk among poor folks in San Francisco, I do not see the sleek black limousine occupied by the wealthiest woman in Congress or the wealthiest woman in the Senate. I see disregarded people drifting. Everyone overlooks them, and they know it. They would tolerate chastisement better than being unseen.

I am baffled that our elected representatives refuse to agree on anything, even the size of the negotiating table. They have no arbitrator who will blow the whistle and call foul. They engage in unnecessary roughness and personal fouls during the entire "game." They do agree to be in Washington two days a week for roll call and adjournment for lunch. It would be more tolerable for me if the dapper congresspersons and senators were working in a soup kitchen and had laryngitis. If they were my employees, I would fire them.

I suppose that the poor are so occupied eking out a living that they have no time to organize a revolution, and the parties in Congress provide just enough benefits to keep the poor quiet. The rich control a disproportionate share of the

---

3.   Richard H. Ropers, *Persistent Poverty: The American Dream Turned Nightmare* (New York: Plenum Press, 1991), p. 10.

national wealth. They discriminate against the poor because they do not fear any threats from the lower social class to their monopoly over the nation's wealth. Our representatives in Congress have been ineffective in improving the situation. They spend more funds controlling violence than reducing poverty.

THE CLASS SYSTEM

The class system is one of the causes of poverty in the United States. African Americans have occupied a position lower in the social scale than even the poorest whites. Since poor American whites have the African Americans to look down on, they have not noticed the magnitude of the discrimination against them. By their discrimination against African-Americans, they retain whatever small measure of pride they have.[4]

Well-intentioned religious leaders, educators, and members of Congress unwittingly maintain the status quo of the class system in America. Religious icons are reluctant to speak the truth about the president of the United States, for fear that their followers will criticize them. They blindly support any politician who professes the faith.

The liberal politicians are no better than the conservatives are. Both parties cater to the upper class and give lip service to poor and middle-class Americans. The majority of elected representatives will not jeopardize their livelihoods to be true representatives of the people. The media caters to the wealthy class—those who monopolize the national wealth.

It is not poverty or deprivation in an absolute sense that causes shame, nor is it a lack of material things. Rather, it is a case of psychological deprivation of dignity, self-respect, and pride.

OUR RESPONSIBILITY

Neither Congress nor ungodly American citizens have the capacity to do anything about violence. Only those who honor the lord's commandment have the genuine ability to love the oppressed. Christians can deal with the causes of violence in many ways.

---

4.   Dr. James Gilligan, *Violence: Reflections on a National Epidemic* (New York, Vintage, 1997), p. 199.

The apostle John constantly reminded the disciples of that one commandment he received from Christ himself as comprising all the rest and forming the distinction of the new covenant. "And this is His commandment that we should believe in the name of His Son Jesus Christ and love one another, just as he has commanded us" (1 John 3:23).

The best way for Christians to deal with the excessive violence in this country is to do our best to bestow grace upon others, to help those in need, and to spread the love of God to all we meet.

14

Self-centeredness

Man is as self-centered today as Adam was after his fall from grace. For a detailed discussion on self-centeredness, original sin, and suffering, I urge you to read Arnold Toynbee's book *An Historian's Approach to Religion,*[1] originally written in 1956. Toynbee defines "original sin" as a man's innate desire to be the self-sufficient god, lord, and creator of his life. He sees self-centeredness and original sin as being the same. In the first few sentences of his book, he writes, "Every living creature is striving to make itself into the center of the universe, and in the act, is entering into rivalry with every other living creature, with the universe itself, and with the Power that creates and sustains the universe and that is the Reality underlying the fleeting phenomena."[2]

According to Toynbee, man must walk the road between suicide through self-assertion ("me first") and euthanasia through self-renunciation ("you first"). He describes this road as a razor edge.

I know self-renunciation well. Most of the time, relations and commitment leave me no choice. I use it to survive and to do what is right. It occurs to me that self-renunciation may be another form of doing what is right. It is the love that Jesus spoke about when he admonished me to love my enemies and to bless those who curse me.

I thought that I always chose freely, but now I see that the self might not be involved, and there is only compelled renunciation. In the chapter on love, I said that I often choose unconditional love to the detriment of others and that it is not the right thing to do. Unconditional love is, in essence, forced renunciation.

It also occurs to me that the only healthy kind of renunciation has to be voluntary. Suffering for the sake of love is redeeming; however, suffering that results from forced renunciation is more sinful than self-assertion.

---

1. Arnold Toynbee, *An Historian's Approach to Religion* (Oxford University Press, 1956).
2. Ibid., pp. 1, 4.

In summary, freely choosing renunciation instead of assertion is enough spiritual exercise, and if done to excess, it is equally as self destructive as self-assertion. It would have been better if I had chosen self-confidence instead of self-sacrifice. I now see that being politically correct is another form of foolish forced renunciation. Henceforth, I will be more discriminating and inclined to tell the liars to go to hell.

In the last chapter of his book, Toynbee writes that no soul can avoid the internal struggle between self-centeredness and self-renunciation, but "mankind has never succeeded in unifying the whole of its experience of the universe."[3] He believes that in the atomic age, the spiritual field of activity, not the physical one, is going to be the domain of freedom.

To me, atomic physics is closer to the mystical than any other science. The spiritual is infinitesimal and more understandable to atomic physicists. They can envision galaxies beyond those presently observed. They are more aware of duality and its presence in the soul, so they have less skepticism about the spiritual world.

I am familiar with the spiritual world without the aid of science; I have a greater understanding of the nonphysical world. I have greater freedom in the world, because I believe in a world to come. When I experience tribulation, I do not like it, but it does not stymie me. I go on by the grace of God, which helps me understand and cope with my human condition. My spiritual function is to seek communion with the god behind the occurrences and to seek to bring myself into harmony with eternal truth.

FOLLOWING LOVE'S LEAD

I find it difficult to suffer for the sake of the unrighteous and unenlightened; nevertheless, some individuals choose to do so. This does not mean that voluntary self-renunciation is a fool's choice.

St. Francis let go of the finite realm and sought refuge in the infinite. He believed that he would gain the finite, because for God, all things are possible. He enjoyed earthly things as few people have enjoyed them. He followed love's lead and renounced everything for eternal life. He received the stigmata for his devotion to Christ.

---

3.   Ibid., p. 286.

HEALTHY VOLUNTARY SELF-CENTEREDNESS

Not only are you your brother's keeper for his physical needs but also for his spiritual well-being. It is our responsibility to share the wisdom and experience regarding the pain and suffering that we must endure to follow love's lead. When we recognize the self-centered individuals that show no interest in this path, we must beware of our self-centered desire for the power we enjoy from "saving souls." It is not our responsibility to save or enlighten anyone at the cost of our own souls.

OUR RESPONSIBILITY

Christians must travel the razor's edge between the spirit and the body, remembering that the body is the temple of the Holy Spirit. If self-centered individuals refuse to mend their ways, we should stop abusing ourselves with repressed resentment, anger, bitterness, and hatred. We are better off enjoying the peace of God that passes all understanding.

15

Destiny

People are inclined to think that fate is an inevitable and adverse outcome. *Webster's New World College Dictionary* defines "fate" as "the inevitability of a course of events as supposedly predetermined by a god or other agency beyond human control." *Webster's* lists destiny as one of several synonyms for fate. It defines "destiny" as "a predetermined course of events often held to be an irresistible power or agency; it implies something foreordained and often suggests a great or noble course or end."

OUR DIVINE DESTINY

Our loving and righteous god allows us to be exposed to distressing or unfortunate incidents. There are no accidents. For example, he does not shield me from wicked individuals. If I joined the army, I could be deployed to Iraq and die from a bullet wound. John the Baptist was beheaded by Salome. St. Peter was crucified with his head pointing to the ground. Christian saints were martyred. Wicked people caused these deaths, and God did not intervene, because he allows men to choose between good and evil. Humankind is exposed to the law of causality: everything that exists or happens has a cause. For martyrs and others who believe in eternal life, the greatest tragedy is the rejection of God's plan for salvation and eternal life. The holy spirit within wills and works for his good pleasure. "Work out your own salvation with fear and trembling; for God is at work in you, both to will and to work for his good pleasure" (Philippians 2:12–13).

God has established a set of absolute values, including wisdom, justice, courage, and moderation. I believe that all individuals must work out their own destinies to do his will and that God works with us to do his will. We have free will to choose good or evil, right or wrong. We are not mere puppets or slaves for God. We are co-laborers in accomplishing his purposes.

True happiness lies in our recognition that God is in control of all things. It is comforting to know that I have a magnificent destiny to do his will on Earth, and when I die, I am destined to have eternal life.

Slothfulness, pride, avarice, gluttony, lust, and violation of the Ten Commandments are examples of conduct that are not pleasing to God and result in adverse outcomes. When we sin, we must never give up. We can ask for forgiveness and return to our duty.

DOES AMERICA HAVE A DESTINY?

Without a population, a nation does not have a destiny. It is the people in a nation who give it an identity. When we refer to America, we are not referring to Anglo-Saxons. America is a multicultural nation, and collectively, these citizens are called Americans. For example, it would be nonsense to say that America is English because many of its inhabitants speak English. Many people erroneously believe that America is a Christian nation because there are more churches than synagogues and mosques.

By definition, destiny implies something foreordained and often suggests a great or noble course or end. When there are only a small number of Americans who believe that they have a destiny "to do justice, to love mercy, and to walk humbly with their God" (Micah 6:8), then Americans will have no destiny. I have heard it said that nominal Christians have not even made a microscopic difference on Earth. They come near to God with their mouths and honor God with their lips, but their hearts are far from him (see Isaiah 29:13). They do not acknowledge God, so they have no reason to expect his blessing, and without his blessing, all is nothing.

INDIVIDUALS HAVE UNIQUE DESTINIES

If a great number of Americans have a purpose that is in agreement with an individual's obedience to God's will, the individual is free to participate in the collective destiny. If the national destiny is not in agreement with God's will, the individual is free to reject it.

PREDESTINATION AND PREDETERMINATION

Infallible foreknowledge (predestination) is God's eternal vision of the future; apart from this, individuals are free to resist and reject God's grace. Born-again Christians can and do fall away. When we are tested, we must persevere to the end in order to attain salvation (see Matthew 10:22 and 24:13 and Philippians 2:12–13). God foresees the individual's activity exactly as he or she is willing to form it; therefore, predestination is not predetermination of the human will.

OUR RESPONSIBILITY

Christ is a refuge for individuals who are in need of divine help. We must become like children and open our hearts to God in remorseful confession. We need to acknowledge that we are sinners and in need of grace.

We have the choice between an inevitable and often adverse outcome (fate) and a foreordained course (destiny). When we choose one, we reject the other. If we do not choose destiny, fate will be the determining cause for the events in our lives.

We have a similar choice between good and evil, truth and falsehood, and God and Satan. Frequently, Satan triumphs because of our inaction. It is our responsibility to choose the great and noble course.

16

Discipline

America has fallen on hard times due to a serious lack of discipline. Most people in America want the good life, but are unwilling to exercise the discipline required to earn it. They want blessings, but they do not want to go to the trouble of being truthful, loving, and faithful in order to achieve the blessings they desire.

When I was a child, my parents gave me plenty of positive reinforcement and encouraged me to trust God to guide me through his revealed word. I followed their example and sought similar role models, who also led me along the way of righteousness. I tend to lose patience with people who refuse to acknowledge that they have undesirable character traits.

A person's character traits define him or her. More often than not, you can depend on a responsible and reliable individual. Some people are untrustworthy, and as a matter of course, you cannot depend on them for anything. As a rule, conscientious individuals are more likely to be dependable, and indifferent people are more likely to be untrustworthy. Some people are organized and methodical, while others are careless and disorderly. Some are thoughtful and understanding; others are malicious and cruel.

These personality traits are not just things we are born with, whether we want them or not. Honesty, justice, goodness, kindness, and courage are all habits we can choose to acquire. So are dishonesty, deceit, wickedness, and injustice.

LACK OF DISCIPLINE

The moral character of the majority of Americans today is inadequate. Some value high marks in school more than wisdom; others prefer an impressive résumé to integrity. It is hard work to maintain our personal and natural environments, and many people choose the wide, easy, and polluted life.

This lack of discipline is the result of self-centeredness, more accurately called "original sin." We choose the kind of moral character we want.

NO FREE LUNCH

From my childhood until the day of his death, my father taught us, "No work, no eat." Work requires discipline. I cherish every moment I spent working to pay for my living expenses and my education. Nowadays, the United States government provides addresses and phone numbers of places where lazy people and illegal immigrants can get something for nothing. The saying "There is no such thing as a free lunch" has become a joke, not an admonition.

First, if you are not invited, you do not get a free lunch. This principle applies to everything you or your family members need, including an education. Second, stay away from idle individuals and all freeloading institutions. Note this passage from Thessalonians: "For even when we were with you, we gave you this command: If any one will not work, let him not eat. For we hear that some of you are living in idleness, mere busybodies, not doing any work. Now such persons we command and exhort in the Lord Jesus Christ to do their work in quietness and to earn their own living" (2 Thessalonians 3:10–12).

OBEDIENCE

Self-discipline allows us to do what is necessary when no one else is willing to do it; we make decisions when others are indecisive; we persevere and take risks. Self-discipline helps us evaluate our objectives, avoid what is harmful, and obey God's commandments.

In 1 Corinthians 9:24–27, St. Paul emphasizes that, as followers of Christ, our spiritual lives form the cores of our characters. We are to live as if we are running a race for the greatest prize of all. We must focus our attention on the ultimate goal of the spiritual life and run a disciplined race toward it. We must maintain self-control to be qualified.

The Holy Spirit is the source of self-discipline. As we grow in faith and walk in obedience, we experience greater freedom and pleasure.

SANCTIFICATION

Webster's New World College Dictionary defines "sanctification" as:

1. To make holy; specific, a) to set apart as holy; consecrate; b) to make free from sin; purify

2. To make binding or inviolable by a religious sanction

3. To make productive of spiritual blessing

4. To make seem morally right or binding

A justified, born-again believer has two natures: a fallen nature inherited at birth (Psalm 51:5, 58:3; Ephesians 2:3) and a spiritual nature because of the presence of the Holy Spirit in the heart. (Rom. 8:1–6). The person who accepts Christ as savior and lord is perfect in him, in the sense that Christ is now dwelling in the heart and directing the thoughts, feelings, and aspirations. Sanctification is the daily discipline of accepting and appropriating the power of Christ's Holy Spirit. As we focus our minds on Jesus and reject evil, we "grow in the grace and knowledge of our Lord and Savior Jesus Christ" (2 Peter 3:18). We become aware of him in his word and unite with him in prayer. The Holy Spirit transforms us, and we become more like Jesus.

Through discipline, we rely more fully upon the perfect righteousness of Christ and not upon our own efforts. Christ constantly subdues the power of our fallen humanity, and we experience his presence moment by moment. This does not mean that we can equal the infinitely perfect character of Christ; however, like Christ, we can be kind, merciful, compassionate, and free from sinful behavior.

IT'S OUR CHOICE

One would think that adults would know the meaning of the word discipline. I have my doubts. Many individuals never complete the work they promise to do, because they lack discipline.

Most adults believe they know the meanings of the words love, truth, justice, and faith. I suspect that few use them appropriately in everyday conversation. We hear what we want to hear, and we understand little of what we do hear.

We have some control over our personal discipline. Parents, teachers, coaches, friends, neighbors, spouses, and good Samaritans all have a hand in affecting our moral character.

OUR RESPONSIBILITY

A person who develops a vice or virtue at an early age will probably retain it until death. People seem unable to change their character traits. What is impossible for people is possible for God. When we trust and obey the Bible as the word of God and believe that God is incarnate in Christ, then the indwelling Holy Spirit changes our hearts and minds where wrong outlooks, attitudes, and values exist. It is possible for God to change us when we pursue his knowledge and truth, as I described in the chapter on truth. Only then will there be character reformation in those who trust and obey.

17

Suffering

Some people do not talk about their hardships. They fear that sharing their problems may ruin their image, so they suffer in silence instead of discovering the purpose for their trials.

OUR PERSONAL CROSSES

When I was in North Carolina, Mrs. Fitzpatrick, a devout Irish Catholic widow, frequently invited a fellow officer and me to Sunday lunch. I intently listened as she spoke about her faith. She expressed her belief that each of us had to carry our own personal cross. I had not experienced any suffering to speak of in my early twenties, and I only had knowledge about one cross. Nowadays, we do not hear Christians talk much about personal crosses.

After starting a law practice and a family, I learned all about personal crosses. Each time that I encounter another cross, I vividly remember to the last detail that day at lunch when I first heard about a cross that others, besides Jesus, had to carry.

GOD SUFFERS

When I grieved over the death of my daughter, it never occurred to me whether or not God suffers when I suffer. Looking back, I remembered that Isaiah, referring to Jesus, said, "In all their affliction he was afflicted, and the angel of his presence saved them; in his love and in his pity he redeemed them; he lifted them up and carried them all the days of old" (Isaiah 63:9).

How can it be that God would love the world and give his only begotten son to die for our sins and not have pity on us when we are afflicted (see John 3:16)?

CHRIST SUFFERED

It was fitting that God, for whom and through whom all things exist, in bringing many children to glory, should make the pioneer of their salvation perfect through sufferings.

Hebrews 2:10

Christ learned obedience because of the pain he suffered. Although he was a son, he learned obedience through what he suffered (Hebrews 5:8). Likewise, we learn the purpose of our pain when we face adversity. Suffering is the foundation for making sons of God who reflect their father's character. Suffering made Christ complete as God's son. Christ became the author of eternal salvation because he was willing to learn from the suffering process (see Hebrews 5:9).

BELIEVERS SUFFER

By all outward appearances, I have no reason to suffer. I am financially independent and in good health and sound mind. I have traveled abroad many times, I live in the lap of luxury, and I enjoyed a challenging legal career. Nevertheless, I am profoundly dissatisfied because of man's inhumanity to man. What I write about this is only the tip of the iceberg compared to the chaos I see daily. The primary reason for my suffering is that there is suffering.

My other options were to work from sunup to sundown, to live in a rented house, to abandon the pursuit of knowledge, to play it safe, and to daydream about someday when I would retire. I rejected these options. I took risks and achieved important goals, even though I underwent failure.

When all is said and done, in success and failure, pain and pleasure, there was only one thing necessary: to fear God and keep his commandments. God will bring my every good or evil act into judgment (see Ecclesiastes 12:13–14).

Suffering can be very difficult for the moment; however, God knows when we have learned our lessons. He has promised that he will not try us beyond what we can endure (see 1 Corinthians 10:12–13).

If you can see its purpose, you can handle far more discomfort, pain, and suffering than you may think, with God's help. Our present sufferings are nothing compared to the glory he will reveal in us. Consider this biblical quote on glory:

Therefore I endure everything for the sake of the elect, that they also may obtain salvation in Christ Jesus with its eternal glory. The saying is sure: If we have died with him, we shall also live with him; If we endure, we shall also reign with him; if we deny him, he also will deny us.

2 Timothy 2:10–12

UNBELIEVERS SUFFER

Some suffering is due to sin: humankind's disobedience of God's law. Man has an innate propensity toward wickedness. God created a perfect world, but human beings, in their ignorance of him, cause one another to suffer. Excessive care for the pleasures of the world causes unbelievers to suffer. Here are some examples.

Self-will is a significant source of suffering. Their failure to attain a desired goal triggers pain and anger. Self-pity inundates them with tragic memories, and they believe that no one has ever been so mistreated. Vanity causes them to believe falsely that they are what they would like to be, and this causes conflict and suffering. They may work with wisdom, knowledge, and skill, and then they must leave all they own to someone who has not worked for them. The ultimate sin of pride causes agonizing suffering and despair.

They may have wealth, possessions, honor, and their heart's desire, but they may not be able to enjoy them, and a stranger enjoys them instead. Hypersensitivity is a common source of suffering. Highly sensitive people interpret negatively every word they hear and are offended by the most innocent remarks. Many people grieve under the weight of imaginary offenses instead of forgiving real offenses and disregarding unreal ones.

TALKING THE TALK

In order to live the life of Jesus Christ, his followers must conform to his character of righteousness, purity, and truth. We are to put on the new nature, having been created after the likeness of God in holiness (Ephesians 4:24).

Because the flesh is constantly at enmity with the spirit, putting on the new man requires a daily infilling of the Holy Spirit. Putting our faith in Christ does not instantly give us complete control over our sinful nature. We need to remind ourselves constantly that it is the lord's battle.

WALKING THE WALK

I identify with Job's reaction to the devastating events in his life and his attitude toward God. Though Satan annihilated Job's family and possessions, Job did not attack or blame God. Instead, he showed a submissive attitude and admitted that his blessings had come from the lord. In Job's adversity, he considered his circumstances and learned from them.

In a second encounter, God permitted Satan to assault Job's health, but God retained final control over his life. Satan afflicted Job with boils over his entire body. His wife charged him to curse God. Job considered his circumstances and acknowledged that he gladly received good at the hand of God and had no cause to complain about the evil he received at his hand.

Job understood that the lord has a great purpose for all humankind. He had absolute faith in God's overall control of the suffering in his life. Job knew that the lord was operating in his life and that nothing could impede his purpose.

OUR RESPONSIBILITY

Knowing why we suffer will not eliminate our pain; however, we can explore the benefits that come from suffering.

When we suffer, we learn not to trust in ourselves, but in God. Instead of fighting suffering, we should embrace it when it comes. Focus on the spirit of Christ in you. Forget who you think you are. With the spirit of Christ in us, we can be like Christ (Romans 12:2), and his life can live in and through us.

18

Forgiveness

What is forgiveness? *Webster's New World College Dictionary* defines "forgive" as:

1. To give up resentment against or the desire to punish; stop being angry with; pardon.

2. To give up all claim to punish or exact penalty for (an offense).

3. To cancel or remit (a debt).

Forgiveness is vital for our peace and tranquility. Without it, there cannot be healing for us or reconciliation with others.

GOD'S FORGIVENESS OF US

It is beyond our ability to comprehend how much God loves us. Jesus referred to this ignorance when he asked his father to forgive those who participated in the crucifixion, because they knew not what they were doing (Luke 23:34). When we learn to forgive others, we begin to experience God's love, mercy, and forgiveness for us.

WHEN GOD DOESN'T FORGIVE

God, in his perfect love for us, sometimes withholds forgiveness in certain circumstances. Jesus said that his father will not forgive a man's trespasses if that man does not forgive others (Matthew 6:15). God will not overlook our sins and embrace us until we come face to face with sin and see it for what it is. God's intention is to bring about legitimate shame and repulsion toward sin. The result will be spirit-inspired, genuine repentance and love.

OUR FORGIVENESS OF OTHERS

When we petition God to forgive us our trespasses, we must also forgive those who have trespassed against us (Matthew 6:12). Forgiveness is essential for the fulfillment of Christ's commandment and is necessary in order to maintain a love relationship with God and our neighbors.

How do we deal with the emotional and physical pain we sustain from an offense? If we do not handle the pain of the past in a spiritual way, we will become angry and bitter. We will close ourselves off and withhold love from others.

Forgiveness produces a change in our relationship with the person we forgive. It also allows the party responsible for the injury to be set free. When we are in the process of forgiving others, God brings healing into our hearts.

HOW OFTEN SHOULD WE FORGIVE?

God's love and forgiveness are without limit. Forgiveness is an integral part of love, and without it, there is no love. If we put a limit on the number of times we forgive, we will become self-righteous and proud. When we refuse to forgive one more time, we limit God's grace, love, and mercy to us and our love and mercy to others. In Matthew 18:21, Peter sought Jesus' counsel on this very topic. He asked Jesus, "Lord, if another member of the church sins against me, how often should I forgive? As many as seven times?" Jesus' answer implied that there should be no limit to how often we forgive.

WHOM SHOULD WE FORGIVE?

In the eighteenth chapter of Matthew, we find that we are to forgive everyone. Christ tells a parable about a servant who refused to forgive a debt owed him by a fellow servant: "Then his lord summoned him and said to him, you wicked slave! I forgave you all that debt because you pleaded with me. Should you not have had mercy on your fellow slave, as I had mercy on you?' And in anger, his lord handed him over to be tortured until he would pay his entire debt. So my heavenly Father will also do to every one of you, if you do not forgive your brother or sister from your heart" (Matthew 18:32–35).

Absolutely everyone is included in God's plan for forgiveness; however, self-centered people usually have difficulty forgiving others, asking for forgiveness, accepting forgiveness, and forgiving themselves.

WHEN FACE-TO-FACE FORGIVENESS IS NOT POSSIBLE

Sometimes we are unable to make direct contact with those who have offended us. Perhaps their whereabouts or identities are unknown to us; on the other hand, they may have passed away. Many have experienced suffering due to unfair laws or honest misunderstandings. In such situations, there is no one person from whom to seek reconciliation.

If you cannot personally forgive those who have sinned against you, go before God in prayer and ask him to help you forgive these offenses in your heart. With his help, you can set aside bitterness, hatred, and the natural desire for revenge.

FORGIVENESS WITHOUT REPENTANCE

True repentance is a godly type of sorrow accompanied by transformation. A hardhearted person might not be willing to accept our forgiveness. If the offender has no remorse for his conduct, it is unlikely that there will be rehabilitation. Any offender who does not repent will suffer the consequences of that decision.

Even if the offender does not repent, we satisfy Christ's command to forgive if we do so from the heart. Only by the grace of God can we forgive a person who has no remorse.

OUR FORGIVENESS OF GOD

When someone hurts us, we sometimes become angry with God for permitting the offense. We may stop attending church, reading God's word, praying, or associating with other believers. Some people go so far as to seek lifestyles of sin, becoming involved in drugs, promiscuous sex, or the occult, in a conscious or subconscious attempt to get back at God for the pain they have suffered.

If an individual who is angry with God turns to him in openness and sincerity, he will find love, peace, joy, and forgiveness. As he returns to the loving arms of his heavenly father, and to the embrace of the fellowship of his people, he will come to realize that God is not to blame for his pain. When he accepts the lord's gracious forgiveness, he will learn to resolve his anger against him.

FORGIVENESS IS NOT FORGETTING

Some injuries are so severe that they cripple the victims psychologically and physically. In time, these people may be able to eradicate the bitterness and hatred in their hearts, but it is far more difficult to forget the source of the pain. Only God can give us the grace to forget.

Some memories remain with us; however, we should not permit them to control our attitudes and behavior, even toward those who were responsible for those memories. We do not want the experiences of the past to dominate our future and hinder our relationship with God.

FORGIVENESS IS NOT TOLERANCE

Forgiveness does not mean minimizing a hurtful incident. When the pain is real and the incident was wrong, it does not help anyone to downplay its significance.

Forgiveness does not mean we should not hold people accountable and responsible for their actions. Justice demands that the offenders make restitution to the victim and/or serve time in prison.

OUR RESPONSIBILITY

Satan loves to complicate our understanding. Sin can darken our minds so that we fail to remember the simple, basic message of the Bible: love. Love is the purpose for living. Love alone rules forever.

> *Love never ends; as for prophecies, they will pass away; as for tongues, they will cease; as for knowledge, it will pass away. For our knowledge is imperfect and our prophecy is imperfect; but when the perfect comes, the imperfect will pass away.*

1 Corinthians 13: 8–10

If any one says, "I love God," and hates his brother, he is a liar; for he who does not love his brother whom he has seen, cannot love God whom he has not seen.

1 John 4:20

Forgiveness is an authentic expression of love. It is in harmony with universal love (*agape*). When we forgive, we experience the divine, even in the midst of sorrow.

19

Racism

In Matthew 12:25, Jesus says to his disciples, "Every kingdom divided against itself is laid waste, and no city or house divided against itself will stand." Racism is one of the most obvious, prolific, and dangerous divisions in the United States.

Lady Liberty stands at our eastern shore, proclaiming, "Give me your tired, your poor, your huddled masses yearning to breathe free, the wretched refuse of your teeming shore. Send these, the homeless, tempest-tost to me; I lift my lamp beside the golden door!" But when the huddled masses from other countries arrive in this land of opportunity, what do they find? Hatred and prejudice based on nothing more than their appearance, their language, and the origin of their birth.

Those whose families have lived in this country for several generations tend to forget that if they trace their genealogy far enough, they will see that their ancestors also came from foreign countries. With the sole exception of full-blooded Native Americans, we are all descended from immigrants.

The first foreigners to arrive here were from European countries, such as Britain and Spain, so mostly pale-skinned people settled the original colonies. When those of darker complexions were brought in, they were made slaves, forced to work for the whites, considered to be of less value than their lighter-skinned counterparts, and often perceived as having no value at all other than for free labor.

Today, our country, like no other, is a melting pot of ethnic backgrounds. Those who used to be minorities are quickly gaining ground. With this increase in population, many insist on a hearing and atonement for past wrongs. Some modern citizens of European descent argue that they are not personally to blame for crimes perpetrated on those of other backgrounds, and therefore they are not responsible for their ancestors' actions.

To add fuel to these fires, the acts of terrorism that have assaulted our country in recent years have stirred the fires of bigotry against American citizens who happen to be of Arab or Middle Eastern backgrounds … or who even look like they might be.

My Own Ethnic Crisis

As a boy, I witnessed belligerent individuals threatening physical harm to my father and damage to his property simply because he was an immigrant. Apparently, they hated his religion, skin color, and ethnicity. These people called immigrants disparaging names such as dagos, wops, spics, spades, towel heads, krauts, and wetbacks. Immigrants called natives WASPs (white Anglo-Saxon Protestants).

Most immigrants worked in the coalmines, washed dishes in restaurants, built the railroads, operated small grocery stores, peddled dry goods, worked on farms, and labored at other menial jobs to put food on the table. In cities large and small across America in this era, other immigrants were also entrepreneurs, opening businesses and services to serve both their own and the surrounding communities.

When I was in the military and stationed in the South, decent, intelligent, kind members of the church I attended made racial remarks in my presence. I reminded them that I was from a minority culture and that I had personally suffered shame and humiliation from ethnic slurs.

Racial slurs diminished after demonstrations and the enactment of the Civil Rights Bill, but the class system in America and elsewhere is responsible for bias against the culturally different. Until there is a change of heart, there can be no change of mind.

Some liberals hate conservatives, and vice versa. Ideological differences in the United States seem to have intensified the hatred because of America's involvement in wars. Prejudice has expanded beyond race, color, and religion. Police brutality, profiling, and invasion of privacy are evidence of bias.

Natives and Immigrants

Some narrow-minded judges have distorted the naturalization laws due to racism. Here are some examples.

In December 1913, an immigrant born in Zahle, Syria (now Lebanon), went before a federal district court in South Carolina to establish his right to naturalization.[1] The judge denied his application because he did not meet the racial prerequisites for citizenship established in the 1790 Naturalization Act. This act limited citizenship to "free white persons." The judge argued that those words meant "persons of European descent."

In a February 1914 hearing for George Dow, another Syrian immigrant, the same judge reiterated his decision that Syrians are not entitled to citizenship. In April of that year, in another hearing brought before this judge, he restated his prior argument and refuted definitions of whiteness based on linguistic and ethnographic racial classifications. He stated that "the test becomes mainly one of geography," and Dow was excluded because he was not a European. In his petition for a rehearing, Dow asserted that according to the judge's definition of whiteness, not even Jesus would be eligible for naturalization in the United States.[2]

The Dow decision was contrary to the decisions of three other federal district courts that had granted naturalization to Syrians. In 1923, the United States Supreme Court rejected the logic of the federal district court's decisions.

In a 1942 case before the Eastern District Court in Michigan, the judge noted that "apart from the dark skin of the Arabs, it is well known that they are a part of the Mohammedan world and that a wide gulf separates their culture from that of the predominantly Christian peoples of Europe." He went on to say that "Arabs as a class are not white and therefore not eligible for citizenship."[3]

In a 1944 decision, a Massachusetts federal district judge wrote that "the Arab people stand as one of the chief channels by which the traditions of white Europeans, especially the ancient Greek traditions, have been carried into the present." He granted the petition for naturalization.[4]

On December 15, 1944, in the district court of the United States for the southern district of West Virginia, my father became a citizen. His certificate of naturalization states that his former nationality is "Syrian of white complexion."

Dr. Michael W. Suleiman, a native of Palestine and a professor at Kansas State University, provides a detailed history of Arabs in America over a century. He documents their struggle for acceptance, notwithstanding their contribution and successes. Dr. Suleiman notes: "Despite the fact that Arabs have lived in America for more than a century and despite their major successes, they are still struggle

---

1.   Ex parte Shahid 205 F.812 (E.D.S.C. 1913).

2.   Ex parte Dow 211 F.486 (E.D.S.C. 1914) and In re Dow 213 F. 355 (E.D.S.C. 1914).

3.   In re Ahmed Hassan 48 F. Supp. 941 (E.D. Mich. 1942).

4.   Ex parte Mohriez 54 F. Supp. 941 (D. Mass. 1944).

for acceptance in American society. Full integration and assimilation will not be achieved until that happens."[5]

OTHER PREJUDICES

In addition to ethnic prejudice, this country has an infamous reputation for mistreating various groups of people. African Americans were given voting rights by the Fifteenth Amendment to the Constitution, enacted into law in 1870. Prior to the 1920s, women did not have the right to vote.

Though more severe and widely publicized in other countries, religious persecution exists here as well. Closely related denominations of Christianity fight over minute points of doctrine. Americans ridicule and humiliate others who admit that they have closely held religious beliefs. Far worse, some who openly express their faith have been kicked out of their neighborhoods, have had their property vandalized or destroyed, or have been abused physically or verbally.

Religious fundamentalists ostracize from society people who make choices that are different from the established norm, including prostitutes, unwed mothers, women who have had abortions, divorced people, and those who engage in a same-sex lifestyle. Regardless of whether such individuals have committed a sin (as defined by God in the Bible), their fellow sinners should not punish the people themselves. We are all guilty of some sin or another. With the exception of legal and just repercussions for actual crimes committed against other human beings, the responsibility of establishing appropriate consequences for those who "fall short" belongs to God alone. He is the epitome of justice and mercy, holiness and compassion.

WE ARE ALL FOREIGNERS

We are all sojourners, living on this earth for a limited number of years. Our eternal souls will live on after death, but not here. Those who have accepted Father God's provision for their sins by asking his son, Jesus, to come into their hearts will spend eternity in heaven with everyone else who has made that choice during their lifetimes. Since heaven is our true home, we are all "foreigners" in this world.

---

5.   Michael W. Suleiman, "Arabs in America: Building a New Future," *Arabs in America* (Philadelphia: Temple University Press, 1999).

OUR RESPONSIBILITY

The desire to prove oneself by putting down others is a bottomless pit. God, the creator, has made each of us in his image, and he has chosen the particulars of our ethnic backgrounds, genders, appearances, and circumstances in his infinite wisdom, which is beyond our ability to comprehend.

Envying others who seem to have more than we do is also pointless. Many of those who attain the American dream of fame and fortune find that reaching that goal results in emptiness and grief, not joy and peace. We must learn to be content with who we are and what we have, rather than hating others for the blessings God has chosen to bestow upon them.

Let us ask God for the grace to forgive those who have trespassed against our ancestors or us. Moreover, may we strive to live in harmony with everyone.

PART II
Quest for Certainty

20

Democracy: Theory and Reality

I was a boy of eleven on Pearl Harbor Day. In those days, patriotism was part of the American fiber. I believed that everybody was a law-abiding citizen who trusted in God.

In secondary school, I learned that America is a government of the people, by the people, and for the people. I studied the ideologies of the founding fathers, the Declaration of Independence, the Constitution, and the Bill of Rights. I memorized the phrase about equality that Thomas Jefferson wrote in the opening of the Declaration of Independence.

In college, I learned about the functions and responsibilities of the three branches of the federal government. In law school, I studied constitutional law and the twenty-seven amendments to the Constitution. I was thrilled that the Constitution included statements about equality and that God had endowed me with certain unalienable rights to life, liberty, and the pursuit of happiness. For me, American democracy was always synonymous with freedom.

I started to lose my idealism about this country in the fifties, when I observed segregation and racial prejudice. I questioned how this noble land, under God, could allow such inequality.

At first, when my illusions started to crumble, I refused to accept the discouraging truth. As injustice went more and more out of control, I concluded that my beloved country had a terminal condition.

EQUAL BUT SEPARATE

It was our creator, not Thomas Jefferson or the federal government, who endowed all men and women equally with certain unalienable rights. Yet corrupt federal government, institutions, and individuals, from time to time, deprive men and women of their rights.

During my tour of duty in the military, African-American officers stationed in the South had to use separate water fountains and toilet facilities. If there were none, they drank Coca-Cola and relieved themselves behind trees.

I also noticed the unbelievable poverty of both blacks and whites living in the area immediately adjacent to the military base. I observed physical injury and the deaths of poor people, and, unjustly, the culprits too often escaped prosecution.

Some people believe that such lawlessness has always existed in America and that television has simply exposed the extent of it. I believe that lawlessness resulted from the American class system. The obstacles to equality are the self-righteous government, corrupt institutions, and wicked individuals.

LOSING DEMOCRACY AT HOME

As I understand true democracy, the citizens hold the ruling power, either directly or through their elected representatives. There is equality of rights, opportunity, and treatment.

In this country, however, our elected representatives pass legislation that benefits special-interest groups to the detriment of others. In addition, many voters in southern states acquiesced to the conduct of Strom Thurmond, a senator from South Carolina, and Alabama governor George Wallace. Both were segregationists who denounced federal intervention in the states' right to allow segregation.

Jacques Martin Barzun obtained his PhD from Columbia in 1932 and taught history there from 1928 to 1955, becoming a professor of history and a founder of the discipline of cultural history. According to Barzun, Western democracy, as we have known it, is in decline. The symptoms include a deterioration of the political parties, a decrease in voter turnout, a growing disregard for politicians, and the displacement of politics from the center stage of society. These developments point to a deeper problem incipient in Western civilization.[1]

CAMELOT

Americans vent their spleens when casting their vote for president and rooting for their Super Bowl favorite. Reason goes out the window, and hysteria is in charge of them. They want a wonder-worker for president and another one for an NFL coach, and there are none.

---

1.   Martin Jacques, "Democracy Isn't Working," *The Guardian*, June 22, 2004.

Jackie Kennedy forever changed the presidency from reality to a castle in the sky. She and Theodore H. White, a journalist and a friend of the Kennedy's, memorialized JFK with the show-tune words from Camelot. Her recollections formed the basis of White's *Life* magazine article entitled "For President Kennedy: An Epilogue," which appeared on December 6, 1963.

Richard Burton (who played Arthur in *Camelot*) and JFK were notorious womanizers. This is the only connection between JFK and Camelot. Americans still hope that a return of Camelot would be near. The next presidential debate is near; however, it will not be Camelot. It will be "Here Come the Clowns."

Do you remember Harry and Bess Truman? He was a haberdasher from Missouri who wore a Stetson hat and took a daily stroll. Thank God, he was not like Jack Kennedy.

Gone are the days when the first lady wore a knockoff designer dress and attended a state dinner looking like a housewife. Bess was not like Jacquelyn. There was never an occasion when Bess was at Harry's side on the rear platform of a train, continuously waving her right hand like a pendulum and flashing a silly grin.

Harry accomplished great things without any of the hype that the Kennedys had. He was "Give 'em hell Harry."

Few American presidents were cut from the same cloth as Washington, Jefferson, Teddy Roosevelt, and Lincoln. They were leaders before becoming presidents. Their leadership gave dignity to the office of president. Some of the stooges that followed in recent times sought dignity from the office and brought shame to it.

In the year 2000, a C-Span ranking of all U.S. presidents was conducted by fifty-eight presidential historians and scholars. Harry S. Truman ranked fifth, behind Lincoln, Franklin D. Roosevelt, Washington, and Theodore Roosevelt.

PROMOTING DEMOCRACY ABROAD

In spite of serious problems, the United States is vigorously promoting democracy abroad, making grand efforts to convert other nations into capitalist democracies. Our federal legislators appropriate billions of dollars in foreign aid, in the hope that countries under other forms of government will choose a representative form like ours.

According to Thomas Carothers, a leading authority on democratization worldwide and an expert on U.S. foreign policy, America's democratic principles and standards have been damaged by the torture of prisoners at U.S. facilities in Iraq and Afghanistan, holding persons in legal limbo at Guantanamo Bay, and eavesdropping without court warrants within the United States. A country that tortures people abroad and abuses rights at home should not be telling other countries how to behave.[2]

I do not know of anyone who is interested in promoting democracy in Iraq. I do not approve of our violation of human rights in Iraq. I have all that I can handle in keeping life and limb together at home without sending servicemen to free Iraq and spending billions in such an effort.

Domestic and foreign corporations, under the guise of freeing foreigners, are pressuring the United States to stick its nose under someone else's tent in order to protect American investments overseas. The shah of Iran was not interested in democracy. He wanted financial aid for his enterprises.

According to Sheldon L. Richman, senior editor at the Cato Institute:

> After seventy years of broken Western promises regarding Arab independence, it should not be surprising that the West is viewed with suspicion and hostility by the populations (as opposed to some of the political regimes) of the Middle East. The United States, as the heir to British imperialism in the region, has been a frequent object of suspicion. Since the end of World War II, the United States, like the European colonial powers before it, has been unable to resist becoming entangled in the region's political conflicts. Driven by a desire to keep the vast oil reserves in hands friendly to the United States, a wish to keep out potential rivals (such as the Soviet Union), opposition to neutrality in the Cold War, and domestic political considerations, the United States has compiled a record of tragedy in the Middle East. The most recent part of that record, which includes U.S. alliances with Iraq to counter Iran and then with Iran and Syria to counter Iraq, illustrates a theme that has been played in Washington for the last forty-five years.[3]

Middle class Americans are financing the war in Iraq, sacrificing sons and daughters and pinching pennies so that the wicked corporate officers can receive millions in bonuses. Dick Cheney is one of them. Both political parties are aware of all this and implore God to bless America.

2.   Thomas Carothers, "The Backlash against Democracy Promotion by Foreign Affairs," Foreign Affairs, March/April 2006, as quoted in http://www.carnegieen-dowment.org/publications/index (accessed May 12, 2006).

3.   Sheldon L. Richman, senior editor at the Cato Institute. "Ancient History: U.S. Conduct in the Middle East Since World War and the Folly of Intervention." Cato Analysis No. 159, August 16, 1991.

One last thing—place yourself in the shoes of an average Middle Eastern family. Overall, what would your considered opinion be of America? Would you want to adopt the same morality that exists in the United States today? What solutions would you offer the families? The American ideals of democracy have come to a standstill. So why are we pushing our failed system on other countries?

GOD'S DEMOCRACY

Because Jericho was under Canaanite occupation, its destruction was certain. The Canaanites believed that cultic prostitution was required to encourage their gods to mate, so that rain would come and the land would be fertile. Evil people forced young people into prostitution and often abused them to the point of death. Parents sacrificed their firstborn children by fire to the god Molech. The destruction of the city of Jericho was God's punishment for their sin.[4]

It seems to me that few people are aware of what or who their false gods are. Their false gods may be their vocations, prosperity, pleasure, prestige, or human relationships, if they worship them above the lord. If anything robs them of total dependence on God or becomes a greater passion in our lives, it is an idol. Moreover, idol worship, in God's economy, is deserving of punishment.

Our hardened hearts refuse to accept his absolute sovereignty. We may pray for his blessings but at the same time retain control of our lives. We must not treat God as simply a means of accomplishing our ends. The lord is a jealous god, and he will expose our distorted allegiances that stand in the way of his sovereignty.

GOD'S MERCY AND JUDGMENT

Sin outrages God's infinite holiness today just as it did in the Old Testament, and his wrath is no less now than it was then. Nevertheless, his patience and forgiveness are immeasurable. He gives everyone the opportunity to choose between salvation and judgment.

God warns of his wrath and waits patiently for repentance, but when he acts, he judges swiftly. God gave the Canaanites ample warning that he would destroy their evil culture. He waited four hundred years while Israel was in Egypt. After the Israelites passed through the Red Sea, God waited forty more years while

---

4.   www.theology.edu/canaan

Israel wandered in the wilderness. Jericho had six more days to repent while Israel marched around the city seven times. God permitted anyone who wished to leave the land peacefully to go. God ordered the Israelites to hunt down and kill all the Canaanites who stubbornly remained.

In Joshua, chapter six, we read an account of the Israelites exterminating the city of Jericho. They marched around the city once a day for six days. On the seventh day, they encircled the city seven times. On the seventh time around, the priests blew the trumpets, and God's people shouted. The walls tumbled down.

According to Dr. Bryant Wood, director of the Associates for Biblical Research and one of the leading experts on the archaeology of Jericho, an unusual earthquake is the most likely explanation for the walls' collapse. It allowed a portion of the city wall on the north side to remain standing while everywhere else, the wall fell.

It matters little what the Italian archaeologists did not find in their month-long dig. The evidence is already in. Three major expeditions to the site over the past ninety years uncovered abundant evidence to support the biblical account.[5]

People who lived in blatant sexual immorality, promiscuity, violence, and open debauchery (see Genesis 14) inhabited the cities of Sodom and Gomorrah. According to Jude 1:7, they "serve as an example by undergoing a punishment of eternal fire."

God has provided America with an abundance of prosperity that is the envy of other nations. Nevertheless, in recent decades, Americans have indulged in immorality, blatant materialism, arrogance, and self-love. Judgment day is coming.

Churches in America have lost their distinctive platform to call Americans to repentance. Rarely do preachers today deliver sermons on hellfire and brimstone. I know ministers who campaign for tolerance toward the current Sodomites instead of praying for the deliverance of the righteous in present-day Sodom.

I have mentioned in this book three ministers, and I know by name a shocking number of ministers and leaders who brought scorn upon the name of God in front of the unconverted. In addition, their conduct influenced church members.

---

5.   Bryant G. Wood, "Did the Israelites Conquer Jericho?" Biblical Archaeology Review, March–April 1990.

Rescuing America Is No Longer an Option

And he testified with many other words and exhorted them, saying, Save yourselves from this crooked generation.

Acts 2:40

Individual repentance and faith is all that remains. In the end, I do not believe God will save the United States as a nation.

Our Responsibility

I grieve when I observe the rapid deterioration of the ideals that founded this nation. However, I do not see many others who are troubled or brokenhearted by the corruption, self-indulgence, degeneracy, and immorality in America. In fact, most people excuse the wickedness with an air of indifference and remark that the situation is not as bad as it is seems.

In this time of decadence, I choose to ask God for personal deliverance from this dark age, for both others and myself. To survive this dark age, we must put God first, above all else. We need to seek the truth, live the truth, teach the truth, and be willing to suffer the consequences of following the truth.

21

Who Am I, and Why Am I Here?

Many people have no clue about who they are, who created them, or why God created them. These individuals present to the outside world a false persona. They live behind a façade, because they feel inadequate for the task of essential completeness. It never occurs to them to ask the simple yet essential questions of "Who am I?" and "What is my purpose in life?" We find such people everywhere: at cocktail parties, cultural events, the Oscars. They are also in respected professions, universities, Congress, civic clubs, and even churches.

Life is like a puzzle. Wickedness, lies, injustice, violence, hatred, greed, infidelity, etc. are pieces that do not fit into the big picture—the life that God intended for us. Love, truth, justice, moderation, fidelity, etc. are pieces that do fit into the big picture. Our creator gave us the intelligence and free will to choose between pieces of the puzzle that fit and those that do not fit. Unfortunately, some people, for various reasons, never see the big picture.

KNOWING OURSELVES

We must know who we are before we can begin to consider what we might become. The path we choose is the path we will follow until some circumstance causes us to change. Without careful foresight, we might never get on the path best suited for us.

I grew up in a liturgical church and acquired a strong belief in Christ as the son of God. Knowledge of the gospel was an essential piece of the puzzle of life.

In college, I studied Contemporary Civilizations, History of the Hebrew Commonwealth, The Life of Christ, and Introduction to Philosophy, The Philosophy of Religion, and many other philosophy courses that provided additional pieces of the puzzle. One inspiring philosophy professor taught me how to define myself authentically and spontaneously in relation to the world. What was latent in me developed because of his example and creative presentation. He laid the foundation for my spiritual quest.

PURSING A LIFE OF HARMONY

The philosopher Arthur Schopenhauer, notorious for his philosophical pessimism, theorized that the world is not a harmonious place and human life has no hope of satisfaction; nevertheless, an aesthetic experience and sainthood promise some escape from the torment of life's sufferings. According to Schopenhauer, when we overcome the illusion of our individual existence, the renunciation of the will occurs. When we relinquish our will, we lose the impulse to struggle with others.[1]

I agree with Schopenhauer's conclusion, but I like to state it a different way: "Father, if thou art willing, remove this cup from me; nevertheless not my will, but thine, be done" (Luke 22:42).

I am a child of God, and I am on this earth to do his will. The same is true for everyone.

PURSUING A LIFE OF SUCCESS

In order to validate our vain pursuit for fame and fortune, we give it a laudable title, such as a "search for meaning" or a "learning experience." We would be better off if we realized that there is no carrot, and if there is, it is not worth pursuing. The American dream is like a stick with an elusive carrot. When we find the carrot, it turns out to be a mirage, and we continue our search for the real carrot (the abundant life).

I know a number of people who are searching for Shangri-La, but I know of no one who has found it. On the other hand, I know many individuals who pursue a life of faith, even without knowing what the outcome or consequences will be (see Philippians 4:7).

Often, though, we are not satisfied with the paradise God planned for us. We want to eat the forbidden fruit of the knowledge of good and evil. But the paradise of our own creation will be without eternal hope and full of suffering. The

1. Kathleen Higgins, Schopenhauer: The World as Will and Idea (The Teaching Co. DVD, 2000).

paradise God planned for us also has suffering, but with a purpose—conforming us to his image.

For years, the search for Shangri-La, an imaginary and remote paradise on earth, dominated me. I put off letting go of the pride and selfishness that kept me from God. I finally realized that paradise on earth is not the kingdom of God. I had to abandon my search for Shangri-La and pursue faith.

PURSING A LIFE OF FAITH

Many individuals are not motivated to live lives of faith, because such a life demands the extinction of the desires of the flesh and the crucifixion of the self-centered ego. Faith means trusting in a higher being and not in oneself.

Others are not motivated to live a life of faith because they think it is impossible. Jesus lived a life of faith, of course, but he was God, and he endured death on the cross as a result.

> *Then He (Jesus) said to them, "My soul is swallowed up in sorrow—to the point of death. Remain here and stay awake with Me." Going a little farther, He fell on His face, praying, "My Father! If it is possible, let this cup pass from Me. Yet not as I will, but as You will."*

Matthew 38:39

In Romans 8:35–37, St. Paul declares, "Who shall separate us from the love of Christ? Shall tribulation, or distress, or persecution, or famine, or nakedness, or peril, or sword? No, in all these things we are more than conquerors through him who loved us." In recent times, some people endure abusive relationships, illness, disease, and death in order to live a life of faith.

During the lifetime of Danish philosopher Søren Kierkegaard, Christianity was the state religion of Denmark, and Danes were Christians by virtue of citizenship. Kierkegaard, the founding father of existentialism, tried to make the Christian life of faith all about sacrifice. In his book *Fear and Trembling*,[2] he held up to the Danish Christians the example of Abraham, who was willing to sacrifice his son Isaac because he trusted that God would raise Isaac from the dead. But according to the scriptures, a life of faith is not about self-sacrifice or any other

---

2.   Søren Kierkegaard, *Fear and Trembling* (New York: Penguin Classics, 1998).

act on our part. It is about trust in God's plan for humanity. "Without faith, it is impossible to please him. For whoever would draw near to God must believe that he exists and that he rewards those who seek him" (Hebrews 11:6).

LIFE'S ULTIMATE QUESTIONS

We are all on a quest to answer the ultimate personal identity question: "Who am I?" The Bible provides the ultimate answer: "Your body is a temple of the Holy Spirit within you, which you have from God" (1 Corinthians 6:19).

The second question we all ask ourselves is "What is my purpose?" God's word also answers that question: "You are not your own; you were bought with a price. So glorify God in your body" (1 Corinthians 6:20).

God created us for a divine and holy purpose: to glorify God with our lives.

RISING ABOVE OURSELVES

Immanuel Kant was a philosopher of the 1700s. His goal was to formulate universal laws about what is good or right. He accepted as true that we must be willing to rise above our desires and purposes, just as scientists must be willing to rise above their particular biases to find the objective laws of nature. When we do this, we can adopt appropriate principles of action and encourage others to follow them.

Kant introduced the "kingdom of ends" in his book *Groundwork of the Metaphysics of Morals.*[3] This moral philosophy requires that we act toward all rational beings like members of a society in which everyone is worthy of being treated well. It also presumes that we have the free will to do so.

Kant's categorical imperative—that all rational beings are worthy of being treated with respect—was not original to him. The "kingdom of ends" is a statement from the Sermon on the Mount (Matthew 5–7).

---

3.   Immanuel Kant, *Groundwork of the Metaphysic of Morals* (Cambridge University Press, 1998).

OUR RESPONSIBILITY

I can say with reasonable certainty that God created me for his purpose. I urge you to give some thought to the "big picture." If any pieces of the puzzle do not fit, throw them away. Seek the wisdom of people who have genuine faith in the paradise of God that is not of this world.

22

Man's Search for Meaning

I'm always chasing rainbows,
Watching clouds drifting by!
My schemes are just like all of my dreams,
Ending in the sky!

Some fellows look and find the sunshine;
I always look and find the rain!
Some fellows make a winning sometime;
I never even make a gain, believe me.
I'm always chasing rainbows,
Waiting to find a little blue bird in vain![1]
(Words and music by Joseph McCarthy and Harry Carroll, 1918)

Many people wander around aimlessly, looking for the bluebird of instant satisfaction. A few eventually win fame or fortune, but most never make any worldly gain. Those who do reach "the top" often find that it is not everything they thought it would be or that there really is no "top."

Man is constantly searching for meaning, but he does not always know where to go to find it. Others think they have found it, only to discover that what they thought was their unique purpose in life was merely the result of forcing into existence what they thought would make them happy.

---

1.   "I'm Always Chasing Rainbows," words and music by Joseph McCarthy and Harry Carroll, 1918.

MY SEARCH

For years, I searched for meaning and purpose in my life. I believed I deserved the American dream of fame, fortune, power, and perhaps a movie contract or an appointment as chief justice of the Supreme Court. Eventually, I realized that the search for meaning is nothing but a fantasy.

When my relentless search for meaning in the world failed, I sought silence within, away from the senseless, hollow chatter that inundates this world. But this spiritual quest only increased my insecurity.

I finally had to acknowledge the uncertainty of human existence and my utter dependence on God. Instead of a spiritual victory, I needed spiritual poverty, mercy, and meekness. I needed to rely on an omnipotent god, not certainty in this world. Those who have found their purpose in God no longer chase rainbows. In both success and failure, they grow.

EXAMINING OUR LIVES

In Sophocles's play *Oedipus Rex*, Oedipus was living a happy, fruitful life, but he did not examine his life until he learned what fate would someday befall him. Thereafter, he examined his life, suffered his fate, and found the implications of his birth. What would his life have been like if Oedipus had not discovered his true origin?

It is not enough for us to examine our lives. We must also discover the right way to live our lives.

THE ONGOING SEARCH

The fulfillment of our needs is not a once-and-for-all experience. It is a moment-by-moment, hour-by-hour dependence on God to do his will in us.

> *Search me, O God, and know my heart! Try me and know my thoughts! And see if there be any wicked way in me, and lead me in the way everlasting!*

Psalms 139:23–24

STOP SEARCHING

Meaning is not something to be acquired, nor is it something we discover. It reveals itself only when we stop searching for a purpose that meets our personal expectations. When we are in pursuit of "the good life" (carnal pleasures), the creator cannot reveal to us the meaning for which we yearn.

For most of my life, I chased my elusive dreams (rainbows); however, now that I have matured, I wait for the rainbow to find me. At all times, God's spirit works gently within me and does more than I ask. God does the same for all those who allow him to reveal himself to them. His purpose for your life is all that matters. Everything else is an illusion.

OUR RESPONSIBILITY

The search for meaning is more than an intellectual one. The answer must come from heaven. We must be willing to submit to the purpose of our almighty creator and allow him to examine us.

People who do not believe in God can have a purpose in this temporal life, but that purpose will die with them. People who believe in God have an eternal purpose.

23

What Is Love?

I hear a lot of talk on the subject of love, and it seems to me that people know more about physical love (*eros*) than they know about God's love for humanity (*agape*) or brotherly love (*phileo*). Most people do not know how to love God, their neighbor, or themselves, and they do not know how to let God or anyone else love them; consequently, they do not realize that God loves them. They have the capacity to talk about love, sing songs about it, and sometimes pray for it. But they have no clue what love is, so they are lost in a loveless world, speak half-truths, and live a charade.

A LOVELESS WORLD

One evening while I was in New York, I went with family and friends to Times Square. I observed the crowd around me. People of every race and culture meandered aimlessly, spellbound by the neon signs and the hawkers. As I walked among them, I felt sad and empty. I wondered how many were aware of their despair, seeking love to fill the mysterious emptiness they felt. The hawkers and the sponsors of the neon lights offered a moment of thrill, inevitably accompanied by a lifetime of disappointment.

GOD'S LOVE

Because the world observes that many of those who trust in God have no money, no favor, and no honor, it does not believe that God is love. In the eyes of the world, those who serve material wealth or possessions have power, possessions, and every comfort. How presumptuous, secure, and proud they are because of their possessions, and how despondent when their possessions no longer exist or are withdrawn. The world does not know the ultimate end of those who do not trust in God.

We cannot love God in a vacuum of ignorance. We must know in our hearts that God is of great strength, a proven deliverer, and a tremendous comfort before we will trust him to be our all in all. But when we know that, our knowledge about God controls our emotional responses.

The heart is the center of thought, attitude, understanding, and knowledge. The mind keeps God's law, his commandments, his statutes, and his judgments. No one is above the law; therefore, grace does not cancel a believer's obligation to obey the Ten Commandments. Instead, grace increases the obligation. Everything depends on obedience, which is love in action.

God's son, Jesus Christ, is the ultimate example of perfect love. Out of love and pity for humanity, he chose to suffer in order to show others the path to absolute reality. He had the option to avoid crucifixion and claim his divine status, but he relinquished his divinity to save others.

LOVING OTHERS

"Love is patient and kind; love is not jealous or boastful; it is not arrogant or rude. Love does not insist on its own way; it is not irritable or resentful; it does not rejoice at wrong, but rejoices in the right. Love bears all things, believes all things, hopes all things, and endures all things." These words from 1 Corinthians (13:4–7) ring true to us even today; why else would they be so often recited at weddings?

The apostle Paul believed that love is the greatest of all good, and the pain and suffering that Christians must undergo for following love's lead is not too high a price to pay.

ANALYZING LOVE

I obtained most of the following analyses on the subject of love from Robert Brown's book *Analyzing Love*.[1] According to Mr. Brown, the first problem is to identify how love differs from liking, benevolence, and sexual desire. What kinds of objects can we love, and what judgments and objectives does love require? Second, there is the problem of recognizing the basis for claiming that love is present

---

1.   Robert Brown, Analyzing Love (Cambridge University Press, 1987).

or absent in particular cases. The third problem is comparing love with fear and anger, contrasting the emotions with attitudes, and finding an appropriate place for love with respect to these categories.

Mr. Brown asks if we need to justify our love. Do we have reasons for loving, display judgments in love, and find a basis for criticizing the judgments and evaluations made by lovers of the objects of their love? Lovers may or may not know the basis for their judgments.[2]

TYPES OF LOVE

Romantic Love

I distinguish romantic love from infatuation, and I can like someone without a desire to be intimate with them. With immediate family and relatives, I want them to be trustworthy, unselfish, responsible, and conscientious. I try to help form, maintain, or change the character traits of my family.

When I was courting my wife, I was charmed by her presence and made despondent by her absence. For me, this is evidence of love. Furthermore, if the flame is still there, lovers continually express their love for one another.

In Theodor Fontanne's novel *Effie Brest*, the heroine, an engaged girl named Effie, discusses her forthcoming marriage:

> I'm all in favour of equality. Love and tenderness of course, as well … Love comes first, but immediately afterwards comes luxury and a position in society; after that comes entertainment—yes, entertainment. Always something new, something that will make me laugh or cry. The one thing I can't stand is boredom.[3]

According to Mr. Brown, there are three types of infatuation. In the first, blind desire and unfamiliar forces carry away the lover and leave her or him without evaluative judgment. In the second, the lover has an uncontrollable craving for whatever he or she does not prefer and considers unworthy. In the third, the lover is ignorant and reckless. The person's unsound appraisals of fact or value, or the inability to affect the craving by appraisals, or both, affect all three types.

---

2.   Ibid., p. 11–12
3.   Theodor Fontane, *Effi Briest* (London: New English Library, 1962), pp. 17–18 as quoted by Robert Brown, *Analyzing Love* (Cambridge University Press, 1987), p. 75.

These three types form the difference between "the passion of infatuation and the passion of thoughtful love."[4]

I see them everywhere, in parks, in restaurants, in shops, strolling along on Broadway, and at open-air concerts. They are starry eyed and holding hands, and they do not have a care in the world. As Satchmo used to say, "Let's fall in love." Who am I to say otherwise? But is it love or just infatuation? Unfortunately, no one seems to know the difference.

In past times, society expected Southern belles to marry by age eighteen. Nowadays, some marriage counselors and attorneys advise singles to wait until they are twenty-five or thirty years old before tying the knot. I got married at the tender age of thirty.

As expected, the divorce rate is higher among couples who marry in their twenties. Mothers panic when their daughters are approaching thirty and are not married. The financial burden must shift sooner rather than later; otherwise, there might be trouble ahead.

You will soon learn that infatuation by any other name is a fantasy. It is biological, and love is logical. There can be love without it, and I would rather skip infatuation.

The florist, jeweler, seamstress, caterer, baker, musician, travel agent, finance agent, organist, soloist, photographer, limousine driver, and tuxedo rental agent know that it is only a matter of time before the smitten individuals will be knocking at their doors. You will observe that I did not mention marriage counselors. First off, the father of the engaged couple or the less fortunate couple will soon be in debt because of the forthcoming wedding and cannot afford counseling. Second, many sessions will be needed to discover each individual's ability to assume a role in marriage. Finally, they might find out that they would have serious differences in marriage. It is best that parents urge the lovesick individuals to see a doctor and, if necessary, use the wedding funds to pay for it. In time, society will be better for it.

Marital Love

Later on, I will discuss the ideal marital love. For now, I identify it as one type of love, and I will state the essentials for an enduring and harmonious marriage.

Compatibility is mandatory in a successful marriage. During courtship, couples place the "urge to merge" ahead of ascertaining whether they are compatible. This is concealed and usually not apparent.

---

4.   Robert Brown, *Analyzing Love* (Cambridge University Press, 1987)., p. 38.

I have observed that relationships fail for at least two reasons. First, individuals cannot choose compatible partners during courtship. Second, words and conduct are not trustworthy. Once married, people may behave differently than while in courtship. According to data for the 1994 National Center for Health statistics, for every two couples who married, one will call it quits The devil and the evil urge have imperiled the sacrament of marriage and the family. The nation's values crumbled when American family life declined. Consequently, children of failed marriages have come to believe that the risks outweigh the benefits in marriage. They avoid entangling alliances and prefer group social life to dating.

Parental Love

Children learn by example, participation, and instruction. They learn the attitudes of love, pride, shame, tolerance, conciliation, and even hatred. Caring adults should know their role in marriage and teach children how to love. Most parents know more about self-assertion and selfishness than about self-renunciation. Remember what Abe Lincoln once said: "A house divided cannot stand."

Gratitude

An authentic love relationship requires a grateful heart. An ungrateful person does not have the joy of a grateful heart.

In Luke 17:15–17, Jesus healed ten lepers, but only one returned to thank him. Jesus inquired where the other nine were. "Was no one found to return and give praise to God except this foreigner?" Those who did not return to thank Jesus took his generosity for granted. To the one who did return in gratitude, Jesus said, "Rise and go your way; your faith has made you well" (verses 18–19). The faith of this leper made him well. Because the other nine had no faith, God did not heal them.

Supernatural Love

The love that Jesus talked about is supernatural and impossible to accomplish in our own strength. But in Christ, we have the capacity to care about the well-being of others to the same degree as we care about our own well-being, or to an even higher degree. The apostle Paul talks about a power to love that God makes available to us when he states, "I live; yet not I, but Christ lives in me" (Galatians 2:20).

UNCONDITIONAL LOVE

Webster's New World College Dictionary defines "unconditional" as "without conditions or reservations; absolute." It must be unrestricted by human feelings or failings.

Many secular psychologists argue that people must give (and should expect to receive) unconditional love with no demands. They claim that everyone is born with the right to unconditional love. They contend that people experience emotional and behavioral problems if they do not receive unconditional love. Others argue that people are not able to love unconditionally and that those who believe they love unconditionally are only deceiving themselves.

God is love, and his love is unconditional, but does that mean God must bestow his love on everyone, even unbelievers? If God loves unconditionally, are we to do the same?

A large number of respected Christian leaders have adopted the teaching of unconditional love and acceptance. They believe that God commands us to unconditionally love and accept one another and that it is contrary to biblical teaching to demand specified performance or good behavior. They conclude that people should love and accept others and themselves unconditionally because God loves and accepts them unconditionally.

We must investigate these basic assumptions by considering God's revelation of himself in his written word. Are we to love everyone indiscriminately, all the time, regardless of his or her destructive behavior?

UNCONDITIONAL ACCEPTANCE

Does unconditional love require unconditional acceptance? Christians who believe that they must accept others unconditionally are compelled to suffer evil in every aspect of their lives in the name of Christian love. They forfeit their right to reject all behavior that is contrary to biblical teaching. In addition, parents who accept the idea of unconditional acceptance must tolerate everything their children do and the lifestyles they choose.

When we study the issue of unconditional acceptance, we must consider God's holiness and his justice. God's incomprehensible love does not explain his reaction to disobedient men who conspire to betray him and his son. Those who teach unconditional acceptance also ignore the law of God: the Ten Commandments. We cannot keep them without God's help.

In my opinion, the divorce rate among Christians is good evidence that couples are uninformed about the connection between the love for God, the commandments, and the love of one another. If a Christian does not know the commandments and the teachings of Jesus, then he or she cannot know about *agape* (spiritual compassion). Keeping the commandments is the only way to demonstrate our love for Jesus, God, others, and ourselves.

I am convinced, beyond a shadow of doubt, that I could not know anything above love unless I had a personal relationship with Jesus. Keeping the commandments is essential for life and love. Consider that Jesus said to his disciples, "He that hath my commandments, and keepeth them, he it is that loveth Me: and he that loveth Me shall be loved of My Father, and I will love him, and will manifest Myself to him" (John 14:21).

The prodigal son's father waited and hoped that his son would repent, but he did not extend his love until the son repented (Luke 15:11). This story illustrates the vastness of God's love, forgiveness, and mercy, but it is not an illustration of unconditional acceptance. The restoration of the father-son love relationship required that the son discontinue his evil pursuits. God knows what the prodigal sons are doing. "He that sitteth in the heavens shall laugh: the Lord shall have them in derision. Then shall he speak to them in his wrath, and vex them in his sore displeasure" (Psalm 2:4–5).

To the cities that refused to repent, Jesus said, "Woe to thee, Chorazin! Woe unto thee, Bethsaida! For if the mighty works, which were done in you, had been done in Tyre and Sidon, they would have repented long ago in sackcloth and ashes. However, I say unto you, it shall be tolerable for Tyre and Sidon at the Day of Judgment, than for you. And thou, Capernaum, which art exalted unto heaven, shalt be brought down to hell … it shall be tolerable for the land of Sodom in the Day of Judgment, than for thee" (Matthew 11:21–24).

Unconditional acceptance of all persons deprives us of individual freedom. It distorts our understanding of the nature of justice within the family and in our relationships with individuals, institutions, and ourselves. God is, by nature, righteous, just, holy, compassionate, and incomprehensible. God must remain true to his nature.

UNCONDITIONAL SALVATION

Some Christians believe that unconditional love leads to unconditional salvation. If repentance is a requisite for salvation, does that mean God's love is conditional?

I know virtue when I see it, and I know evil when I see it. I also know the techniques for ascertaining whether an item presented as a fact matches reality. That is all I need to know in order to understand that God is loving, just, merciful, compassionate, munificent, and righteous. This being so, I know that God is true to his nature; in other words, he will be just.

I also know right from wrong and sinful from sinless. God is omnipotent (all-powerful), omniscient (all-knowing) and omnipresent (all-pervading, everywhere). He has no form or limits. Although I cannot fathom who or what God is, I know he exists and that he rewards those who seek him.

I also know that many are called, but few are chosen (Matthew 22:14) and that there will be a time of judgment. All of this has been written in scriptures, including the statement that God wills that none should perish. Despite the fact that God's love is unconditional, we must repent of our sins and take on his nature as a condition for salvation. In other words, we cannot go to heaven if we do not believe that Jesus died as atonement for our sins and that a just God imputes to us the righteousness of Jesus.

> *For by grace you have been saved through faith; and this is not your own doing, it is the gift of God not because of works, lest any man should boast.*

Ephesians 2:8–9

Some refuse his grace, and others choose to receive it. But an act of will is not work. God requires repentance and enables us to grow in righteousness. We cannot partake of God's love if we do not repent. If this were so, salvation would be for all people.

Those who insist on unconditional salvation from God ignore his righteousness. Jesus died for our transgressions, not for our right to continue living ungodly lives. God gives eternal life to those whom he has enabled to believe in his son. Jesus washed away our sins. Whoever does not believe in Jesus as the only begotten son of God shall not inherit eternal life and cannot partake of God's love. Men are required to have faith prior to salvation by grace.

DESTRUCTIVE LOVE

Christ's parable of the good Samaritan answers the question "Who is my neighbor?" Love requires that we provide for our brother's physical needs and give spiritual guidance to nurture his soul. But extending God's love to others does not require us to destroy ourselves in the process. It accomplishes nothing for the giver or the taker when the taker rejects the love offered and continues to destroy himself and the giver.

God does not expect us to love everybody indiscriminately all the time, regardless of his or her destructive behavior.

GIVERS AND TAKERS

For the sake of discussion, I will identify two classifications of individuals: "takers" and "givers." Takers expect everything for nothing. They have a childish fantasy that the giver's sole purpose in life is to make their dreams come true. Personal tragedies do not seem to make takers conscious of their behavior. Takers are manipulators. They have an insatiable need to win.

Takers have never learned how to give. They have no clue what love is, and they have no interest in the welfare of anybody but themselves. They are lazy, self-centered individuals who do not have the energy and capacity to place the interests of another above their own. Often, takers are loath to express gratitude to anyone for unearned privileges, because they think they are entitled to them.

Scarlett O'Hara, the heroine in *Gone with the Wind*, is a classic example of a psychological taker. She does not have the capacity to give selfless love. Eventually, her husband, Rhett Butler, does not give a damn about her.

Givers have a problem similar to that of takers, but with less manipulation. Givers often give out of a sense of unworthiness or guilt. Givers who feel uncomfortable receiving from others do not understand that love requires responsiveness. There is great harm when we do mindless acts that only cause others to become bitter.

UNGRATEFUL RECIPIENTS OF LOVE

Let us assume for a moment that benefactors, out of a sense of duty, guilt, covenant, or mercy, place the interests of undeserving and unpleasant beneficiaries above their own. If the beneficiaries do not enhance the benefactors' pleasure and happiness or their ability to think and act, their arrogance and self-righteousness creates negative emotions. The beneficiaries assign the benefactors a villain's role and falsely assassinate their character. These beneficiaries have no clue about what authentic love is.

Judging Love's Recipients

Must we sanction wickedness in order to respect an individual's right to choose his or her destiny? The recipients of unconditional love will be inclined to continue in the error of their ways. Instead of repenting, the recipient's pride accelerates, and she or he will reject God's love.

> *My children, do not ignore it when the Lord disciplines you, and do not be discouraged when he corrects you. For the Lord disciplines, those he loves, and he punishes those he accepts as his children.*

2 Corinthians 4:17–18

Embracing the Leper

We all have inner conflicts between individualism and our innate need for unity with God and humankind. In order for us to have a sense of community and experience the joy and love of God, we need to "embrace the leper."

For me, the "leper" is anyone with whom I am not compatible. This includes manipulators, people who demand that I be what they want me to be, those who will not let me be who I am, and people who lack discipline or who demand unearned privileges.

Is it possible to embrace all "lepers" at all times? Let us suppose for a moment that the leper is someone who seeks to destroy all that you hold sacred. Is it humanly possible for you to go along with ideologies or behaviors that are contrary to all that you are? Is it possible to follow Christ's admonition to love our enemies, to the point of our extinction? Are we to be tolerant to the extent of approving the conduct of those to whom we grant the freedom to be what they want to be?

The answer to these questions depends on the kind of leprosy we are embracing. We can choose to embrace a person with a repulsive physical condition over which he or she has no control. It is more difficult to embrace a person who has a repulsive state of mind or behavior over which he or she refuses to exercise self-control. It is to my detriment and theirs to embrace character traits and conduct that are objectively repulsive.

OUR RESPONSIBILITY

Jesus' disciples asked him, "Teacher, which is the great commandment in the law?"

He replied, "You shall love the Lord your God with all your heart, and with all your soul, and with all your mind. This is the great and first commandment" (Matthew 22:36–38).

God, the only eternal good, wishes to draw us to himself and away from everything else that exists. The first commandment requires true faith and trust of the heart that settles on the only true god and clings to him alone.

Diligently examine your heart and find out whether it clings to God alone. If your heart renounces and forsakes everything that is not God, then you have the only true god. If your heart does not take refuge in him, then you have another god.

It is our choice whether to have eternal blessing, happiness, and salvation, or eternal wrath, misery, and woe. We can ask for nothing more than his promised blessings, protection, and help in all our needs.

24

Marriage

Some people who marry never knew much about true love or the responsibilities of marriage. In addition, during courtship, many misrepresent their qualifications for marriage and the depth of their commitment. This deception has caused a tremendous upheaval in the family structure of our country, which is one of the major causes for its downfall. In chapters four and five, I covered the subjects of truth and falsehood. In this chapter, I will discuss deception in relationships, specifically in the stages leading to and including marriage.

DECEPTION IN RELATIONSHIPS

Deceit in any relationship is subtle and usually goes unnoticed until someone discovers a specific act of unfaithfulness. Only then do they see the lies and the underlying causes for them. Most individuals are reluctant to confess their lies. Even if they do, they may refuse to admit that the lies caused any great harm to others.

DECEPTION DURING THE ENGAGEMENT

For decades, I have witnessed that couples will spend more time planning the ceremony and honeymoon, selecting the engagement ring and wedding dress, and preparing bridal showers and bachelor parties than they will meditating on the sacredness of their marriage vows. Nowadays, some engaged couples attend premarital seminars and counseling. Ironically, many seminar leaders and marriage counselors are divorced. Exemplary role models are few.

Deception in Weddings

I have an uneasy feeling at weddings, because there is too much pageantry and a great deal of fantasy. An untold number of brides are fixated on their "dream weddings"; I will refrain from identifying any brides. Another male could substitute for the groom, and many brides would hardly notice the difference. In a recent television commercial, the groom departed, and the best man married the bride.

In my opinion, a private, inexpensive family ceremony is sufficient. The father of the bride would serve humanity better if he gave the money to charity instead of spending it on an extravagant display. In 1961, our wedding cost me less than three hundred and fifty dollars, including the gown and reception (nonalcoholic punch and cookies).

People are usually aware that they have certain character traits that could hinder them from fulfilling their responsibilities in marriage, but they take the marriage vows anyway. Some individuals confess later that they did not love their mates when they married.

I do not claim that many people lie when they take their marriage vows. Some people merely take the vows irresponsibly. They might not have the intent to deceive; they simply believe they know more about the requirements of marriage than they do.

Deception in the Wedding Vows

The promises made in most marriage vows, whether traditional or customized, include certain key words; in sickness and in health, for richer or for poorer, for better or for worse, as long as they both shall live, couples vow to love, respect, honor, cherish, support, be honest with, be faithful toward, share their happiness with, and be trustworthy to each other. Yet, according to the U.S. Census Bureau, as of December 1998, 19.4 million adults were divorced, representing 9.8 percent of the population, as compared to 3.2 percent in 1970 and 8.3 percent in 1990.[1]

---

1.   Terry Lugaila, "Marital Status and Living Arrangements," *Current Population Reports*, December 1998, as quoted in http://www.census.gov/prod/99pubs/p20-514.pdf (accessed July, 2006)

In January 2007, my wife and I will have been married for forty-six years, and there has been tension, conflict, and fatigue from the struggle for martial survival.

DECEPTION IN MARRIAGE

There are a lot of behind-the-scenes remarks and jokes by husbands and wives about married life, but few, if any, are willing to admit that their own marriage is in trouble. Women who have affairs often claim that boredom and lack of romance drove them to the extramarital relationship, even though they claim to love their husbands. I say that is nonsense. The spouse who says, "I love you, but I'm bored and need an affair," is telling a lie. No one who breaches the marriage covenant through adultery can possibly be genuinely in love with anyone but her or himself.

Mature married couples demonstrate love by fulfilling each other's needs. In enduring marriages, honesty, respect, integrity, and faithfulness are valued more than riding off into the sunset with someone.

American psychiatrist Harry Stack Sullivan gives a practical definition of marital love: "When the satisfaction or the security of another person becomes as significant to one as are one's own satisfaction or security, then this state of love exists."[2]

LOVE AND MARRIAGE

You cannot have marriage without love. Nevertheless, many couples marry when they are not right for one another, and consequently, few experience authentic love. It is apparent to me that people get married for many reasons other than love.

One reason that comes to mind is the urge to procreate. Their passion causes them to be reckless, hasty, and careless in getting married.

Another reason is some women's urgent need for someone to take care of them. This is not as prevalent today as it was when women could not prepare for and obtain high-paying positions. In a male-dominated work environment, women without college degrees would be inclined to find someone to take care of

---

2.   Harry Stack Sullivan, *Conceptions of Modern Psychiatry* (New York: W. W. Norton & Co., 1953), as quoted by William J. Lederer and Don D. Jackson, MD, *The Mirages of Marriage* (New York: W. W. Norton & Co., 1990). p. 42–43.

them. Over fifty years ago, women whose families could afford the cost went to college to get their "Mrs." degrees. But even today, many women seem to prefer a day at the mall to exposing themselves to the stress of an eight-to-five job. In the stressful and laborious conditions they encounter at work, some men are chomping at the bit to reverse roles and give the ladies a crack at fame and fortune.

MARRIAGE HYPOCRISY

A marriage is only as authentic as the individuals involved, and so it is with civilizations. Hypocrisy is part of the cloth of self-righteousness, and together they are part of the garment known as the false self.

In preceding chapters, I constantly mentioned the human condition (original sin) that is the root cause of the decline of individuals and nations, and so it is with marriage. All of us have darkness within, and we need light from some other source.

Everyone wants and needs love; however, many people do not know how to love. Consequently, they pretend to love others, including their spouses, and they unconsciously commit destructive acts against them.

As I stated before, in America, the masquerade is everywhere, and it is difficult for a person to meet people who know the source of authentic love and can appropriate it and pass it on to others. Authentic love and marriage require two selfless individuals whose egos are submissive to the creator and source of love.

EXPECTATIONS AND DISAPPOINTMENTS

I disagree with hypocritical and naïve people who suggest that there will be no disappointments in a marriage if there are no expectations. If there were no reasonable expectations, neither the marriage nor the individuals would change for the better. Repressing disappointment is damaging to a relationship. I expect a great deal from myself, and I am disappointed if I do not meet my expectations. The same principle applies to my relationships.

In a healthy marriage, husbands and wives can be dissatisfied in their marriages. Before they married, they hoped for desirable qualities in their potential spouse. If they find that those qualities are not present, they may be dissatisfied; however, it is not injurious to the marriage. It can be an opportunity for growth.

Furthermore, a self-centered spouse may find it difficult to accept the challenge of acquiring desirable qualities or relinquishing unreasonably hoped-for ones.

NECESSARY ROLES IN MARRIAGE

From experience, I learned that I have a role in all relationships. As a father, my role is to nurture, love, provide for, teach, and care for my children. As a son, my role is to honor my father and mother, care for them in old age, and assume financial responsibility for myself as an adult. As an employer, my role is to pay adequate benefits and salaries promptly. As a citizen, my role is to serve my country in times of war, pay my taxes, and abide by the laws. The roles I assume are endless.

There are necessary roles in marriage, and they will vary with the circumstances. For a marriage to succeed, each spouse must be receptive to changing his or her attitudes, actions, and temperament. Marriages fail because individuals neglect to assume necessary and reasonable roles in marriage.

AGREEMENT

As an attorney, I learned the art of negotiation. Nowadays, effective negotiators make every effort to have all parties receive an honest result, rather than get the upper hand. Married couples would do well to learn the art of negotiation. Generally speaking, there are many unresolved issues in most marriages. Both individuals strive to get what they want, rather than make concessions.

Furthermore, there is no such thing as martial bliss without conflict. No matter how much we might love and care for our mate, there is bound to be conflict; therefore, we must devise a plan for handling the daily conflicts.

In the Vietnam negotiation, the diplomats spent months simply arguing over the shape of the negotiating table. Many people have criticized this as a remarkable piece of stupidity. Under the circumstances, the debate over the shape of the negotiating table was perfectly rational. This example teaches us that one spouse might think an issue is important while the other thinks it is trivial. We must always try to see a conflict from the other person's point of view.

If you agree with the foregoing analysis and advice, then remember to be steadfast in resolving your differences each day.

In legal negotiations, a disinterested mediator is present to facilitate a resolution. In marriage, the genuine desire to set aside personal preferences and do what is right is enough to resolve most issues. The mediator must have the power to bind the parties; otherwise, the dispute might be unsuccessful.

QUID PRO QUO

I first heard of the term "quid pro quo" more than fifty years ago, when I was a student in law school. According to *Webster's New World College Dictionary*, it means "something given or received for something else." As a founder and partner of a law firm, I had experience with the need for reciprocal behavior, and I instinctively knew that reciprocity is essential in any relationship.

I recommended quid pro quo to my wife early in our marriage, but I encountered some difficulty in convincing her of its value. She said it was irreverent to refer to the holy state of matrimony as a partnership.

Imagine my surprise when William J. Lederer and Don D. Jackson, MD, authors of *The Mirages of Marriage*, recommended quid pro quo in marriage relationships. According to the authors, two people in any close relationship expect reciprocal behavior.[3]

Without quid pro quo, one party could receive all of the advantages and leave the other side empty-handed. In order to resolve disagreements, both parties in a dispute must benefit; otherwise, the empty-handed party will be inclined to terminate the relationship.

DESTRUCTIVE QUID PRO QUO

Common sense dictates that one spouse should assist with tasks commonly performed by the other; however, I observe that many self-centered individuals are lazy, ignorant, irresponsible, and unable to give "something for something." They want their hardworking spouse to support them in the style to which they have become accustomed, so that they can wholeheartedly embrace a life of leisure. For example, it is not uncommon for one spouse to earn a substantial amount of money while the other spouse enjoys unearned privileges. One case comes to mind in which the wife is a highly successful real-estate broker and earns over half

---

3.   Ibid., pp. 285–291.

a million dollars a year. The husband spends most of his time playing golf or duck hunting.

In our affluent society, the spouses of successful professionals and officers of major corporations have no need to earn income. They are free to spend their time supporting the arts, socializing, or shopping. Frequently, in this type of marriage, they have nothing in common. It is a marriage of convenience.

THE REAL CAUSES OF DIVORCE

Jesus spoke against selfishness, lust, vanity, self-centeredness, and treachery. These are the elements of nearly every divorce. When couples do not integrate the sacred and the secular, then there is a greater probability of divorce.

Marriage is a covenant between a man, a woman, and God (Malachi 2:14–16). God created marriage as a lifelong covenant (Matthew 22:23–30) that reflects his love for his people (Hosea 3:1). Any deviation from his decree harms a marriage and violates God's command. (Mark 10:11–12).

No commitment is greater, more obligatory, and more solemn than marriage. In order to fulfill this commitment, husbands and wives need to clarify what their responsibilities are and communicate frequently about the many relationship issues that arise.

In Ephesians 5:31, we learn that a man shall leave his father and mother and be joined to his wife, and they will become one. He is to love his wife as himself. Nothing is said about her doing likewise, but it does say in verse thirty-three that she is to respect her husband.

In Colossians 3:10, the husband is reminded that he has put on a new spiritual nature, which is being renewed in knowledge after the image of its creator. Although it is not mentioned that the wife has done likewise, it is understood that she too has put on a new spiritual nature.

Imagine for a moment that the one flesh created by the joining of a husband and wife is a third self that has put on a new spiritual nature. The old personalities and habits of the man and woman are put in check by the new nature. There is only one new spiritual creature from the union.

If this couple obtains a divorce, then there is a strong probability that they did not become one; they brought into the marriage their old selfish carnal selves. Any relationship takes time, lots of work, sacrifice, and selflessness. In a marriage, it is not easy for the individuals to renounce their old habits and to seek that which is in the best interest of the other.

In my opinion, it is difficult for individuals to be selfless in a materialistic culture. Some individuals who watch television may go into a trance in response to seeing the lifestyles of celebrities. They think that they need another relationship in which there is a possibility that their fantasy will come true. Lederer and Jackson said, "It takes courage to shake the status quo, but if the relationship isn't worth a risk to improve it, it is bound to be forever limited and burdened by its own stagnation."[4]

THE FOUNDATION OF A MARRIAGE

Many single people think that their married life will not have the same conflicts they witness in other marriages. Once married, they are surprised that there are endless conflicts, and they do not have any way of resolving them. For a marriage to survive the intense storms of life, I know that it must have a stable foundation. Foolish people build their marriage on lies. The wise build their marriages on God, the creator of marriage and the embodiment of truth, and he does not fail.

Most people do not expect their marriages to fail, yet many do. One or both individuals are not truthful with God, themselves, or each other. They may be deceptive about their personal relationships with the lord.

PROTECTING YOUR MARRIAGE

I want to share with you some truths I have learned from scripture and from other people regarding the process of fulfilling one's wedding vows. These principles will not guarantee marital bliss; much depends on the spiritual maturity, character traits, and compatibility of the individuals involved. However, they can help you keep your marriage intact, surviving, and even thriving. They apply to all other kinds of relationships as well.

Seek God's Help

Find out what God has in mind for your relationship with him and your marriage. You can obtain this knowledge by the diligent study of the Bible, prayer, and attending church with your spouse.

---

4.   Ibid., p. 219.

Studying the Bible with mature Christians, listening to Bible-based sermons, and reading scholarly expositions of the scriptures will give you the foundation necessary for living the Christian life and maintaining a Christian marriage, assuming that you are willing to apply the truth obtained from these sources.

Resist Satan

Husbands and wives need to flee temptation. Close friendships with the opposite sex can lead to infidelity and the destruction of a marriage. A wise spouse will avoid potentially dangerous situations and intimate conversations with friends of the opposite gender.

In Genesis 39, we read that Joseph's brothers sold him into slavery, and merchants took him to Egypt. There he became the property of Potiphar (37:36), an officer of the pharaoh and the captain of the guard. Potiphar's wife "cast longing eyes on Joseph" (verse 7). He refused her advances, because he had learned a powerful set of convictions in the presence of God. Joseph recognized the consequences that the sin of adultery would have on his relationship with God (verse 9). Sensual pleasure was not worth the disastrous results.

When Potiphar's wife finally got Joseph alone, he ran from her, even leaving his coat behind. He did not fool around with sin, argue with it, or reason with it. He fled from it.

Potiphar's wife lied to her husband about the event (verses 16–18), and Joseph ended up in jail for doing the right thing (verses 19–20). But his relationship with God remained intact, and the lord was with him, even in prison.

Work through Conflicts

Many people have the notion that marriage is supposed to last for a lifetime, yet they conduct themselves as though it is a temporary convenience. Satan can ensnare even Christian marriages. Couples must depend on the biblical promises of God in order to fulfill their wedding vows. It is difficult to keep God's gift of faith in our lives. We must seek it daily; otherwise our memory of it will fade away when the forces of evil confront us.

Seek Professional Help

If you have followed all of the appropriate steps and your marriage is still in trouble, make an appointment with a licensed counselor or psychologist. Depending on God's help does not exclude counseling. On the contrary, he often uses those in the psychiatric profession to help couples work through their problems and find happiness in their relationships.

In recent times, many individuals have turned to psychological testing services to find compatible mates. Television commercials abound with testimonials about finding the ideal mate in this manner. It is almost like saying that the service guarantees that the tested individuals are sinless. Compatible individuals will have conflicts, and they must have a plan to resolve them. Two lazy, self-centered people may be compatible, but they may not know how to struggle for marital survival.

OUR RESPONSIBILITY

If you are contemplating marriage, I urge you to spend plenty of time finding out about the spiritual and personal character traits of the one you intend to marry. Before you take your vows, determine whether or not you are truly compatible. Resist the temptation to get married on the false assumption that you cannot live without him or her. Trust me, you can.

If you are already married, do not be alarmed when tension, conflict, and fatigue occur in the everyday battle for marital survival. Instead of avoiding such things, learn from them. Your character develops with adversity, and God will honor your dedication and perseverance.

25

Teaching the Truth

In America, as in other Western civilizations, hearts have grown dull, ears are hard of hearing, and eyes close in sleep. We do not even know what we do not know! The philosopher Ludwig Wittgenstein wrote, "There are indeed things that cannot be put into words. They make themselves manifest. They are what is mystical ... What we cannot speak about, we must pass over in silence."[1]

Wittgenstein realized the limitation of words in describing truth, and this awareness is essential in education. Educators should confess that they actually know very little about the mysteries of God and the world. Rather than deny their existence, they should pass over in silence those things that they cannot put into words.

Wittgenstein's wisdom is not dominant in our educational system because many educators are worldly, not spiritual. They are scientific, logical, and rational. On the other hand, there are some educators, mentioned below, who integrate the secular and the sacred—the wisdom of heaven and earth.

It is my purpose to identify the shortsightedness in education. This shortsightedness brought about the decline of education and that of our culture.

WHAT WE DON'T KNOW CAN HURT US

According to Mary Midgley, an English philosopher and author, much of what we believe to be knowledge is nothing more than useless information that, after accumulation, is stored in some archive.[2] We need, says Socrates, to grasp both

---

1. Ludwig Wittgenstein, "Tractatus Logico Philosophicus," Lecture 7, as quoted in The Literary Wittgenstein by John Gibson and Wolfgang Huemer (New York: Routledge, 2004), pp. 2, 300.
2. Mary Midgley, Wisdom, Information and Wonder: What is Knowledge For? (New York: Routledge, 1989).

sides of an argument as our own, to feel the force of both, and to direct the whole of it toward the truth, regardless of which side gets the victory.[3]

God formed truth in all of us, yet truth is personal within each of us. We all have a hunger to know God and to be at one with him.

Others have exposed me to many opinions that they would have me believe are truths. My quest for truth has been difficult, because I have spent a lot of time looking for a place, person, school, church, profession, relationship, or experience where I could find truth. I had this hunger, but had no idea how to satisfy it. I did not know the function of the soul. I wandered in the wilderness for years, searching for someone to show me the way to know God.

I am on a quest for certainty, and so are many others. We want God to assume responsibility for our lives. Freedom of choice is a burden, but we can accept the responsibility with reasonable certainty about God's plan for us. In addition, we can rest on his promise that he is guiding us. The best that I can do is to feel the fear and do it anyway.

It is a struggle to know the truth and even more difficult to teach the truth in a culture where people have been taught to believe lies about almost everything.

TODAY'S EDUCATORS

Didaskalos, the Greek word for "teacher," means "one who is fitted to teach, or who thinks she or he is." *Pseudodidaskalos* is the Greek word for "false teacher."[4] The apostle Peter used this word in Peter 2:1: "False prophets also arose among the people, just as there will be false teachers among you, who will secretly bring in destructive heresies, even denying the Master who bought (was crucified for) them, bringing upon themselves swift destruction."

Teachers need to know more than just the subjects they teach. They must also know how to distinguish truth from illusion, know their inward selves, and get to know the students' inward selves. Before they can evoke the truth that students have within themselves, teachers must know the truth they have within themselves.

Another important thing is to give up the self-oriented life. Would-be teachers must give great thought before choosing this honorable vocation.

---

3.   Ibid., pp. 244–245.

4.   Frederick W. Danker, Greek-English Lexicon of the New Testament and Other Early Christian Literature, third edition (University of Chicago, 2000).

THE ORIGIN OF TRUE JOY

Despite the fact that my education integrated the secular and the sacred, I still have difficulty being joyous in a world filled with conflict and misery. For this reason, I pursue the sacred. Had I not been exposed to the sacred, I would not have any clue where to find some joy in the midst of sorrow.

I have grave doubts that the million people in Times Square, New York City, on New Year's Eve and the billions elsewhere in the world know anything about the state of grace. I am in need of this state, as is the entire world.

In his book *Finding Perfect Joy with St. Francis of Assisi: 30 Reflections*, Dr. Kerry Walters writes, "We experience perfect joy when we are in a state of grace … When we enter into perfect joy, we likewise see the good—the God—in everything around us … Even though we may suffer, we still see only good/God in all these tribulations because our state of grace allows us to see with God eyes. And to see only good/God is to be overjoyed, even in the midst of pain."[5]

If knowledge of a loving creator is not the primary purpose of education, then much of what we believe to be knowledge is nothing more than useless information that, after accumulation, is stored in some archive. While on earth and before we die, the greatest fun (false joy) we experience may be wearing silly hats, blowing horns, and possibly proposing marriage in Times Square on New Year's Eve.

THE TEACHER'S TASK

Webster's New World College Dictionary defines *educe* as "to draw out; elicit." The educator's responsibility is not to fill the student with facts but to draw out or elicit truth from the student.

In high school, I was an outstanding student, because I memorized facts and regurgitated them in an examination. My secondary education had nothing to do with eliciting truth from me.

In college, some professors filled me with political science, sociology, economics, biology, chemistry, etc., and I did not store the information. I simply forgot it. A few other professors elicited truth from me. I still remember, apply, and expand on truths that they elicited from me.

---

5.   Kerry Walters, Finding Perfect Joy with St. Francis of Assisi: 30 Reflections (Atlanta: Charis Books, 2002). pp. 87–88.

Law school education was different from high school and college. Professors did not elicit truth from me, and memorizing was of limited use. I analyzed a given set of facts to find legal issues bearing on the rights and obligations of the parties involved. In some sense of the word, I was trained to represent clients and obtain legal justice (truth) based on the given facts.

Fifty years ago, when I was in law school, there were no courses in ethics or professionalism. Perhaps law schools assumed that students had the character and virtues to practice law. But there was adequate evidence that some lawyers and judges, as officers of the court, did not have the character and virtue to practice law.

In my first jury trial, I encountered a dishonest lawyer who corrupted the testimony of a witness who provided a contrary statement to my investigator. I impeached the witness and prevailed in the case. A short while later and unrelated to the above case, the governor appointed the dishonest lawyer to be judge of the superior court. I disqualified him in my client's case, on the grounds that my client would not receive a fair trial.

Professionalism and ethics in the legal profession have steadily declined during my forty-five years of practice. Watergate is only one example of attorneys disbarred for unethical conduct. In 2001, the United States Supreme Court disbarred President Clinton from practice before that court because of his criminal conduct in the Lewinsky matter. The Arkansas Supreme Court suspended him for five years because of perjury in the Paula Jones case. He paid a $25,000 fine.

Some time ago, my law school included mandatory courses in professionalism and ethics. I created a scholarship for students of the highest moral character so that they could become leaders in their legal communities, when it came to values, ethics, and professionalism.

By reducing truth to objective terms, we put ourselves beyond truth's reach. Thomas Merton said, "The purpose of education is to show a person how to define himself authentically and spontaneously in relation to his world—not to impose a prefabricated definition of the world, still less an arbitrary definition of the individual himself."[6] In other words, the main goal in education is to enable the individual to discover who he or she is, discover what the world is, and discover his or her place within the world

In the brief history of my education, some of my teachers knew the purpose of education and showed me how to define myself; I cannot say that any teacher imposed an arbitrary definition about who I am. Others seem unable to define

---

6.   Thomas Merton, *Love and Living* (New York: Farrar, Straus and Giroux, 1979), p. 3.

themselves in relation to their world and reduced truth to subjective terms. Fortunately, the best teachers in my formal education and elsewhere influenced me.

Because of the integrated secular and sacred education I received, I am capable of distinguishing between good and bad education and evaluating right from wrong. I am not a professional educator, but I taught law clerks and associates about their responsibilities as officers of the court. I taught my children about the truths revealed in the scriptures. More importantly, I can distinguish the carnal mind from the author of truth, the Holy Spirit.

Obedience to Truth

You shall know the truth, and the truth shall set you free, according to John 8:32. Most of us are not free, because we have not been obedient to truth. I think we are in bondage to one thing or another and probably know little truth.

I suspect that many individuals have no notion of what is necessary to learn the truth. One thing is for sure: not many teachers know that the goal of liberal education is to liberate us through knowledge. Furthermore, there must be the right type of knowledge, not just information acquired and stored.

We must be obedient to truth in order to know it. We must make an effort to discover it. We cannot acquire it through gradual absorption. I have in mind the discipline of dialogue between individuals who are searching for the mystical truth that will set us free.

TRUTH IN EDUCATION

In the mid-1800s through the end of the 1900s, many missionary-minded men and women established colleges and seminaries so that future generations would learn more about Christianity and be ambassadors for Christ in all parts of the world. The Catholic Jesuits and other holy orders established outstanding colleges throughout the world.

In the early 1960s, Vatican II allowed greater freedom to Catholic laity and priests to engage in dialogue with clergymen of other religions. Onto the scene came priests, ministers, rabbis, authors, medical doctors, psychologists, and philosophers who shared firsthand experience and ancient wisdom about the function and care of the soul. They assumed the responsibility of nurturing the spiritual lives of millions. They published books, conducted seminars, and counseled countless individuals.

Doctors on this spiritual quest challenged the medical profession with alternative medicine. People from almost every occupation and profession attended "body and soul conferences." Starved souls in need of spiritual education purchased untold millions of books.

Colleges and graduate schools today publish glowing reports about the high quality of students and education; however, I have personally witnessed the wicked competitiveness, blatant dishonesty, and rude manners of business people and professionals.

GAPS IN OUR EDUCATION

When I was in law school, several students had degrees in architecture, engineering, chemistry, physics, psychology, and sociology, but they had little knowledge of the arts or the humanities. As a result, many lawyers today do not have any understanding about their responsibility to present "the truth and nothing but the truth."

A friend of mine, the president of the San Francisco Board of Education, once asked me to participate in the California Governor's Conference on Education. I was a moderator in a group of high school students, and I discussed with them the deficiencies in their education. One student said, "We are taught how to make a living, but we are not taught how to live."

In my opinion, we are dumber than we used to be, and colleges/universities inflate grades. Administrators pressure teachers to give students higher grades than are justified so that the student will not leave, resulting in a loss of needed income from tuition.

In his book *This Noble Land*, James A. Michener observed, "I believe that the basic strengths of our nation are such that we can survive as a world leader till about the year 2050. Our kinetic power, already in action, will carry us forward for half a century. I doubt we could make enough errors in that time to hinder our forward motion. So I am what you might describe as a near-term optimist."[7] There are a few in Washington courageous enough to state in public the same forecast as James Michener; however, they are not members of Congress. We only see the tip of Washington's chaos and failure to do anything.

I am not as optimistic as James Michener is, and I am inclined to be a realist. Events are happening quickly, and America no longer has the opportunity to win

---

7.   James Michener, *This Noble Land: My Vision for America* (New York: Ballantine Books, 1997), p. 102.

the hearts of those people throughout the world who have no hope of survival. I think that James Michener's forecast of fifty years is extremely optimistic.

INTEGRATING SPIRITUAL AND SECULAR EDUCATION

Some present-day colleges give their total attention to analysis and reason and no attention to the sacred. Consequently, they cast out an indispensable means for individuals to see others, the world, and themselves anew. Private colleges must integrate secular and spiritual education. A college graduate who does not know about the spiritual nature of a human being is in some ways ignorant. The colleges' failure to nurture the spiritual life of students is apparent in the breakdown of morals in American society, broken homes, drug and alcohol addiction, and the egotistical and hedonistic lifestyle of our culture.

OUR RESPONSIBILITY

With some degree of prudence, I make the following suggestions for integrating spiritual and secular education.

I recommend that a course on the world's religions be included in the curriculum of every college. Huston Smith, author of *World's Religions*[8] and past chair of the philosophy department at MIT, teaches philosophy at the University of California, Berkeley. Some colleges use this book in a course of the same name.

Books about the soul should be mandatory reading. *Care of the Soul*[9] and its companion volume, *Soul Mates*,[10] both written by Thomas Moore, are excellent examples. Mr. Moore teaches how to see others, the world, and ourselves anew, through stories, myths, images, and dreams. His books have practical wisdom, deep feeling, and much love.

---

8.   Huston Smith, *World's Religions*, (Harper San Francisco 1991).

9.   Thomas Moore, Care of the Soul A Guide for Cultivating Depth and Sacredness in Everyday Life (Harper Perennial 1994).

10. Thomas Moore, Soul Mates: Honoring the Mysteries of Love and Relationship, (New York: Harper Perennial 1994).

PART III

Resurrection

26

Religion Is Not God

I have lost patience with those who say that God does not exist and that only a fool could believe in the myth of a divine creator. I am a well-informed student of the Old and New Testaments, and I proclaim, with humility and respect, the good news of God's love and forgiveness.

WHAT IS RELIGION?

According to *Webster's*, religion is belief in a creator, an expression in conduct and ritual, or a system of ethics and philosophy.

God is a divine or superhuman power to be obeyed and worshiped as the omnipotent (all-powerful), omniscient (all-knowing), and omnipresent (all-pervading) creator of the universe.

WHAT IS FAITH?

When I was a child, God was my father. He was my protector, guardian, and counselor. I knew the Ten Commandments at an early age. I had a childlike trust and purpose. I had a strong desire to do the right thing. I gained strength from a belief that God loved me in the same way my father loved me. I was happy doing my schoolwork, working to providing for myself what my parents could not provide for me, and saving my pennies. God helped me do that and more.

As an adult, I prevailed over my adversities. I experienced God's silent but powerful presence in my suffering and tribulation.

Even as a youth, I did not think that it was unusual for my faith to be tested. In my adult life, I was blessed to have the testimony of righteous men whose faith had been tested far beyond mine. When I was going through the testing, I thought that I had little faith; nevertheless, it was sufficient to see me through.

On reflection, I realized that it is not the size of the faith that mattered, but that it exists. In Peter 1:7, we read the purpose for genuine faith: "So that the genuineness of your faith, more precious than gold which though perishable is tested by fire, may redound to praise and glory and honor at the revelation of Jesus Christ."

WHO IS GOD?

Who is the god who gave me the courage and strength to persevere? The third chapter of Exodus gives us the answer:

> *Then Moses said to God, "If I come to the people of Israel and say to them, 'The God of your fathers has sent me to you,' and they ask me, 'What is his name?' what shall I say to them?"*
> *God said to Moses, "I AM WHO I AM." And he said, "Say this to the people of Israel, 'I AM has sent me to you.'"*
> *God also said to Moses, "Say this to the people of Israel, 'The Lord, the God of your fathers, the God of Abraham, the God of Isaac, and the God of Jacob, has sent me to you': this is my name for ever, and thus I am to be remembered throughout all generations."*

Exodus 3:13–15

No one knows the mind of God. French philosopher Blaise Pascal (1623–1662) boldly makes this point: "By faith we know God's existence. If there is a God he is infinitely incomprehensible, since, having neither parts nor limits, he has no proportion to us. We are then incapable of knowing either what he is, or whether he is."[1]

WHO IS CHRIST?

Christ expanded the meaning of the Ten Commandments and established a new covenant. "But this is the covenant that I will make with the house of Israel after those days, says the Lord: I will put my law within them, I will write it on their hearts; I will be their God, and they shall be my people. No longer shall they teach one another, or say to each other, 'Know the Lord,' for they shall all know

---

1.   Pascal's *Pensées, Part III*, trans. W. F. Trotter (New York: Dover, 2000).

me, from the least of them to the greatest, says the Lord; for I will forgive their iniquity, and remember their sin no more" (Jeremiah 31:34).

OUR RESPONSIBILITY

When we symbolically receive the new covenant through Christ's death and resurrection, we resolve to die to our old way of life, to be symbolically buried with him in the waters of baptism, and to rise again to newness of life. In this way, we put on Christ. With him, we partake of the covenant feast of bread and wine (communion). In addition, we share in the promise of God that all nations will be blessed in Abraham and his seed (Mark 16:15–16; Galatians 3:26–29).

27

The Kingdom of God

Civilizations cannot repent, inherit eternal life, and experience God's kingdom here on earth and in heaven. Only individuals can.

The lord does not want us to be concerned about the things of this world. He wants us to lift our focus and concentrate on his kingdom. In Luke 12:29–31, we read: "And do not seek what you are to eat and what you are to drink, nor be of anxious mind. For all the nations of the world seek these things; and your Father knows that you need them. Instead, seek his kingdom, and these things shall be yours as well."

I must admit that although I have a higher standard of living than many others have, I spend too much time thinking about what I will eat, drink, and wear. But in Matthew 6:34, we read: "Do not be anxious about tomorrow, for tomorrow will be anxious for itself. Let the day's own trouble be sufficient for the day."

According to these verses, if we were to find the kingdom of God and his righteousness, we would never be anxious for anything. If Jesus commanded us to seek the kingdom of God, there must be a way for us to find it.

WHAT IS IT?

Paul describes the kingdom of God on earth as "righteousness, peace and joy in the holy spirit" (Romans 14:17). Our understanding of the kingdom of God develops as we follow his word, the Holy Scriptures, and mature in our faith. We can experience the kingdom of God when we allow him to direct our lives through his word.

WHERE IS IT?

If we were to believe what we see on television, in the movies, and in advertisements, the "good life" is here and now. But if we look beyond the hype, we realize that peace and goodwill on earth is merely a fantasy.

This elusive kingdom of God is "in the midst of you," but there are still many individuals who think that it is somewhere in space. In Luke 17:20–21, we find this often-quoted verse that gives us Jesus' answer:

> Being asked by the Pharisees when the kingdom of God was coming, he [Jesus] answered them, "The kingdom of God is not coming with signs to be observed; nor will they say, 'Lo, here it is!' or 'There!' for behold, the kingdom of God is in the midst of you."

What Does It Look Like?

Our society is so full of sin, corruption, and hypocrisy that I'm not sure we would recognize the kingdom of God if we saw it. We have become inseparable from the world and distracted by it.

A scribe asked Jesus, "Which commandment is the first of all?" (Mark 12:28). Jesus answered, "The first is, 'Hear, O Israel: The Lord our God, the Lord is one; and you shall love the Lord your God with all your heart, and with all your soul, and with all your mind, and with all your strength.' The second is this, 'You shall love your neighbor as yourself'" (12:29–31). When one scribe affirmed what Jesus said, Jesus replied, "You are not far from the kingdom of God."

We are close to the kingdom of God when we love God with our entire being, and when we love our neighbors as ourselves.

How Can We Find It?

The parables of the treasure in the field (Matthew 13:44) and the pearl of great price (Matthew 13:45) illustrate that we must give up all allegiance to the kingdom of darkness in order to enter the kingdom of God. The kingdom of God is inherently linked to God's righteousness. How can sinful man be righteous? The apostle Paul stated, "I have been crucified with Christ; it is no longer I who live, but Christ who lives in me; and the life I now live in the flesh I live by faith in the Son of God, who loved me and gave himself for me" (Galatians 2:20).

Jesus confirmed this by saying, "Truly, truly, I say to you, unless a grain of wheat falls into the earth and dies, it remains alone; but if it dies, it bears much fruit" (John 12:24).

Paul is not saying that we must die physically in order to enter into God's kingdom. Rather, he is telling us that we must die to our wicked, evil, worldly selves and allow Christ to live in and through us. For years, I looked for simple answers to simple questions about God's will and the kingdom of God. Before I die, I want to do God's will. When I die, I want to go to the kingdom of God. As I will explain later, I am now convinced that truth about the world and God is one answer and love is the other answer. My conclusions are clearly revealed in the following two verses. Now, if I have doubts, then I remember that God loves me and abides in me. He will love others through me. As an instrument of his love, I have the capacity to love others, and as I love others, I am loving him. The scriptures are an instruction manual for engaging in warfare with evil.

"In this is love, not that we loved God but that he loved us" (1 John 4:10). If we love one another, God abides in us (verse 12). God is love, and he who abides in love abides in God, and God abides in him (verse 16).

OUR RESPONSIBILITY

The kingdom of God can dwell within us, but only if we seek it through earnest longing and prayer to the father for the gift of his divine love. With his love come eternal life and the things necessary to sustain it in this world and in the next.

28

The Will of God

For years, I diligently searched for God's will in my life. After all, the Bible clearly states that God's will is paramount and has eternal significance. "Not everyone who says to me, 'Lord, Lord,' shall enter the kingdom of heaven, but he who does the will of my Father who is in heaven" (Matthew 7:21).

I tried several of the following methods to determine, with some sense of confidence, precisely what God wanted me to do with my life.

Putting Out a Fleece

> *Then Gideon said to God, "If thou wilt deliver Israel by my hand, as thou hast said, behold I am laying a fleece of wool on the threshing floor; if there is dew on the fleece alone, and it is dry on all the ground, then I shall know that thou wilt deliver Israel by my hand, as thou hast said."*
>
> Judges 6:36–37)

Like Gideon, I prayed that God would give me a tangible sign to indicate which of two careers I should follow. No sign was forthcoming. Later, I learned from the scriptures that the only sign God would give his people would be the sign of Jonah. As Jonah was in the body of a whale for three days before he was freed, so it was with Christ, who was in a tomb for three days before he was resurrected. Christ's resurrection is the only sign needed by man for redemption and salvation.

I never experienced any real assurance with this technique. After all, putting out a fleece can take many contorted forms. I could pull out daisy petals and repeat, "This is God's will. This is not God's will."

I am convinced that putting out a fleece is not the decision-making method that God has given Christians; therefore, I do not seek a sign. Some Christians use this method to find God's will. I caution them that their deceitful hearts can mislead them. Egotistical people frequently follow selfish goals and believe that they are doing God's will.

Prayer

Answers to prayer take many forms, but it is difficult to distinguish between an answer to prayer and the natural progression of events. Thus, while prayer is a vital part of a Christian's daily life, used alone, it is not always an accurate assessor of what God's will for us might be on a daily basis.

Audible Guidance

Some individuals have stated that God has revealed his will to them in an audible voice. Others claim to be able to "sense" what God wants them to do. I believe some of these statements and doubt others. In his infinite wisdom, God guides each individual in a unique way, depending on the situation. But our enemy the devil can imitate God's voice, and our own preconceptions may color a vague "sense" in such a way that we hear what we want to hear. Perhaps two of the best examples I can give are prayers for guidance in the selection of a spouse or making an investment. In both instances, an individual is seeking guidance because he or she has some doubt about the matter. Nevertheless, the carnal mind could tempt the individual to turn a deaf ear to wise counsel and follow a strong urge.

Even when I am praying, Satan will tempt me away from God or make me doubt him. Without God, I cannot do anything, so I am cautious not to take credit for the things I do for God. I must not use God to satisfy myself. For example, others told me to focus on the American dream, and I believed the satanic lie.

When I am convinced that I have learned God's answer to my prayer, I add this petition: "Lord, if it is from you, bless it and cause it to grow, that your body, the Church, may be blessed and edified through it."

"What Would Jesus Do?"

In any given circumstance, an individual can seek guidance by reflecting on the question "What would Jesus do?" If the individual is a mature Christian and knows the Bible well, she or he may be able to surmise the answer based on scripture. But many modern situations do not have a direct parallel to an instance in the life of Christ. Moreover, even those gospel accounts that have some connection to what one is facing today will not be an exact match, because the people, the times, and the specifics are different. In truth, no one really knows what Jesus would do in any particular case. There are obvious exceptions. Jesus would not tell a lie, steal, bear false witness against his neighbor, commit adultery, etc. He would love God and mankind. He would rejoice in the truth.

Listening to Others

I have spent many years learning about evil, ungodliness, and my relationship with God. In my studies, I relied on the interpretations of the Bible by scholars, theologians, priests, ministers, and commentators. I listened to sermons by great (and not so great) clergymen. In addition, I studied the scriptures of other religions, psychology, philosophy, and theology. This study expanded and strengthened my Christian faith, but God's will remains a mystery.

Can We Know?

While the techniques described above may all be helpful from time to time, they do not give solid, unquestionable guidance on discerning God's will. Quite the opposite may be true. They could actually obstruct a person's progress in the spiritual journey. However, I am confident that God has given us the means for knowing his will.

How to Know God's Will

I discovered a way for knowing and doing God's will, to the best of my ability. God does not guide Christians through our senses or worldly information. He guides us through his word and his spirit. (See John 16:13–15 and 2 Timothy 3:15–17.)

God's Word

Through his word, God guided me to the certainty of his will for my life. Although many things about God remain a mystery to me, by faith in the Bible, I know without a doubt what he wants me to do:

> Love my enemies (Luke 6:27).
> Do not swear an oath (Matthew 5:33).
> Do not judge (Matthew 7:12).
> Do not store up treasures on Earth (Matthew 6:19).
> Love the lord, my god, with all my heart, with all my soul, with all my strength, and with all my mind, and love my neighbor as myself (Luke 10:27).

After many years of struggle and anguish about doing God's will, I have put my mind to rest about the search. Genuine love is never separated from the Ten Commandments. St. Paul says that "love rejoices in the right" (1 Cor. 13:6). I share the gospel with others, and I avoid telling others what is wrong with their beliefs. It is equally as important to live in truth as it is to rejoice in the right (truth).

GOD'S SPIRIT

No one can worship and love God until they know him; however, individuals who have a personal relationship with Christ are always making their way toward the truth. God will progressively reveal truth to those who draw near to his holiness and mysteries.

OUR RESPONSIBILITY

Any interpersonal relationship takes time to develop. The same is true of your relationship with God. Take the time to get to know him well. Read his word and study it diligently. You can learn a lot about him by reading his "love letter" to you—the Bible.

Talk to him daily, moment by moment, in every circumstance. In addition, be sure to listen to what his spirit is trying to say to your spirit.

Spend time with others in the family, those who know him intimately and love him with all their hearts. Talk with such people about who God is, what he has done, and how he is affecting their lives and yours.

The better you know someone, the more easily you can ascertain that person's likes and dislikes, his wants and desires. The same is true with God. The better you get to know him, the easier it will be for you to know what he wants you to do in any situation of life.

Lastly, there is a popular saying that is helpful if said with sincerity. "It is not about me—it is all about Jesus!"

29

Jesus' Way

For centuries, Jesus has been a sticky point for believers and unbelievers alike. Those who do not believe that Jesus is God incarnate do not know him. Those who do not know Jesus as their lord erroneously think that his teachings are impossible, and they struggle to live a righteous life. A multitude of Christians know very little about Jesus, the incarnate son of God, and absolutely nothing about the indwelling Holy Spirit.

THE MYSTERY OF LIFE

In this passage, Jesus' disciple John reveals the mystery of life: "Jesus answered, 'Truly, truly, I say to you, unless one is born of water and the Spirit, he cannot enter the kingdom of God. That which is born of the flesh is flesh, and that which is born of the Spirit is spirit ... For God so loved the world that he gave his only Son, that whoever believes in him should not perish but have eternal life'" (John 3:1–6, 16).

For me to know the answer to the mystery of Jesus, the embodiment of truth, I had to cross the bridge by faith. Those who choose not to cross cannot know, now or in eternity.

BEING BORN AGAIN

In 1957, my brother and I attended a Billy Graham crusade in San Francisco. Our parents had raised us in the Christian faith, but we had never heard the "born again" message. My brother and I accepted Jesus Christ as our personal savior at the crusade. I truly believed that Christ was the son of God and that he died to save me.

Shortly afterward, it became apparent to me that I had made a personal commitment to follow Jesus Christ. This meant serving God by following Christ's teachings. I was confident that I could live a righteous life, and I believed that God would help me.

Nevertheless, the Bible continually revealed my inability to keep the law. I wanted to experience my new nature, but I was a miserable failure. I was discouraged and defeated every time I tried to keep the righteous requirements of the law. This surprised me, as I could not understand how I could fail with the spirit of God within me. This was my first conscious encounter with my fallen nature.

The apostle Paul had this to say about his efforts to live a righteous life: "Now if I do what I do not want, it is no longer I that do it, but sin that dwells within me. So I find it to be a law that when I want to do right, evil lies close at hand. For I delight in the law of God, in my inmost self, but I see in my members another law at war with the law of my mind and making me captive to the law of sin which dwells in my members ... So then, I of myself serve the law of God with my mind, but with my flesh I serve the law of sin" (Romans 7:15–23).

We must experience that all things are possible with God (Luke 18:27). Otherwise, our lives will remain wretched.

CHRIST'S POWER

Our time on Earth is a series of impossibilities made possible by God's omnipotence. The same divine power that raised Jesus from the dead is at work in us, both to will and to do his good pleasure (Philippians 2:13). Moment by moment, we must be aware of Christ's power to work God's will in us.

Satan, the enemy of Christ and of the followers of Christ, wants to blur our image of Christ. Satan shall have no power or dominion over us.

In one of his sermons on Romans 7:24–25, Andrew Murray said, "God works to will and he is ready to work to do but, alas, many Christians misunderstand this. They think that because they have the will, it is enough, and that now they are able to do. This is not so. The new will is a permanent gift and an attribute of the new nature, but the power to do is not a permanent gift, and it is received each moment from the Holy Spirit. It is the man who is conscious of his own impotence as a believer who will learn that by the Holy Spirit he can lead a holy life."[1]

---

1.   Andrew Murray, "Absolute Surrender and Other Addresses," Sermon 6 (Chicago: Moody Press, 1895).

GOD'S SOLUTION FOR MAN'S SIN

"All have sinned and fall short of the glory of God" (Romans 3:23). But God is holy and cannot stand to look upon sin.

Jesus Christ came to the earth, lived a perfect, sinless life, and died on the cross to save people from their sin. Because we were born with free will, we can choose to accept God's amazing gift of salvation or reject it.

OUR RESPONSIBILITY

What must we do to escape from eternal torture and receive eternal life? How can we obtain the gift made available to us by God's limitless love and Jesus' ultimate sacrifice? There is only one way: Jesus' way.

> *Jesus answered him, "Truly, truly, I say to you, unless one is born anew, he cannot see the kingdom of God."*

> John 3:3

We do not need to strive to be righteous. Our striving is pointless anyway, because no one is truly righteous. Thanks be to God, all we have to do is believe in our hearts and state our faith in words. My training for success in my personal life, in my law practice, and in my church life was a hindrance in my spiritual life. I was trained to be organized, to solve problems, to be conscientious, to try harder, to be self-reliant, to be self-confident, to trust and respect individuals with credentials, to set goals, and to strive with all my might.

In the spiritual realm, we are instructed to rest, to have faith, to obey, and to trust. There are numerous examples of how my training in the secular world was a hindrance; however, I will limit my examples to several. In Philippians 2:13–14, St. Paul instructs the Philippians to "work out your own salvation with fear and trembling; for God is at work in you, both to will and to work for his good pleasure."

After I read the part about working out our salvation, I was off and running. The work ethic served me well in the secular world, and it never failed me. I concluded that God would not object if I put forth my best effort in the project, in spite of the fact that he is at work in me, both to will and to work for his good pleasure. To make matters worse, salvation was not my own doing. "By grace you have been saved through faith; and this is not your own doing, it is the gift of God" (Ephesians 2:8).

I was twenty-seven when I first heard about the doctrine of grace. Before that, all I ever heard was "No work, no eat." Where I come from, there is no such thing as a free lunch, and the doctrine of grace was too good to believe. I was not alone in trying to work my way to heaven. Today, conscientious, intelligent, and mature believers struggle with their egos. I have a suspicion that Satan wants us to work to a point where we become discouraged.

St. Paul reminds us of a joyous way to seek redemption: "If you confess with your lips that Jesus is Lord and believe in your heart that God raised him from the dead, you will be saved. For man believes with his heart and so is justified, and he confesses with his lips and so is saved" (Romans 10:9–10).

Our search for meaning and purpose in life can end this minute. We receive the kingdom of God through birth in the spirit.

30

Eternal Joy

According to the Bible, what are the keys to eternal joy?

RENUNCIATION OF POSSESSIONS

In the parable of the rich young ruler, Jesus indicated that eternal joy is contingent upon renunciation of all worldly possessions (Matthew 19:21). I have encountered difficulty with the theoretical and practical implications of this demand. My carnal aversion to poverty makes it difficult for me to sell everything I own in order to follow Jesus, but I understand that riches can endanger me in this world and the next. Riches, and the increase of them, are the gifts of God, even though I labor for them. God's blessing can become a curse.

My family and I have the necessities and conveniences of life. I saved for emergencies and old age, and we give to the church, to universities, to children's hospitals, for world relief, and to those who are in need. I think that I am a rich man.

In my older years, I am not as attached to wealth as I was in my youth. I have less need for wealth now. I will leave my heirs just enough to educate our grandchildren and for emergencies. I will not contribute to a life of luxury and idleness.

The rich young ruler in Jesus' parable rejoiced in observing the commandments of the lord, but his possessions proved to be the one obstacle to responding positively to Jesus. This attitude jeopardized the man's entrance into the kingdom of heaven. The same could be true for me.

Jesus warned that possessions could prevent us from achieving eternal joy (Luke 12:30). The rich are secure, self-reliant, self-sufficient, and self-satisfied. These attitudes can present serious obstacles to spiritual growth. Jesus often referred to the necessity for concrete, tangible separation from material goods. Here are some examples:

Blessed are you poor; the reign of God is yours.

Luke 6:20

Whoever would save his life will lose it, and whoever loses his life for my sake will find it.

Luke 9:23–24

Renunciation of possessions is a fundamental dimension of the Christian dynamic, because it stimulates receptivity to the kingdom of God. The poor respond most readily to Jesus' proclamations. Jesus indicated that the poor have the free spirit necessary to follow him. But a lack of possessions does not guarantee a receptive heart for the kingdom.

Would life be easier if we held on to all that we have and ignored the poor? Eventually, we would discover that we love our possessions more than we love Christ.

There is another reason that Jesus commanded that we sell our possessions. He wants us to see the futility of self-effort. He knows that, in our own strength, we cannot follow this command. If there is to be any renunciation of our possessions, Jesus must first give us the grace to renounce ourselves.

LIVING A GODLY LIFE

We have an enormous responsibility when we confess before others that we believe in Jesus. But as long as we are in our physical, earthly bodies, our actions will be a mixture of good and evil. Until the spirit subdues our sinful nature, we cannot produce the righteous requirements of the law.

All of us have experienced this conflict with sin. George Whitefield, a minister in the Church of England and one of the leaders of the Methodist movement, said, "My heart is half devil and half beast."[1]

---

1.   George Whitefield, "Christ, the Support of the Tempted," Sermon 19, as quoted in "Who Shall Deliver Me? A Study on Romans 7:20–25" by Dr. Jack L. Arnold Reformed Perspectives Magazine (Third Millennium Ministries), Volume 1, Number 41, Dec. 1999.

In a letter to a fellow prisoner in another penitentiary, John Bradford, an English Protestant reformer and martyr, described himself as "a very painted hypocrite: the most miserable, hard-hearted, and unthankful sinner." You may remember his favorite statement: "There, but for the grace of God, go I."[2]

Bishop George Berkley, an influential Irish philosopher, stated, "I cannot pray, but I sin; I cannot preach, but I sin; I cannot administer, nor receive the holy sacrament, but I sin. My very repentance needs to be repented of: and the tears I shed need washing in the blood of Christ."[3]

It is a normal Christian experience to have conflict with sin, but trying to solve the problem using our own strength will rob us of the joy God longs for us to have. The apostle Paul addressed this paradox in his letter to the church in Rome. He observed the evil urge in his body was at war with his spirit and made him captive. He testified that God through Jesus Christ his Lord save him from the bondage. He serve the law of God with his mind, but with his flesh, he served the law of sin (Romans 7:22–25).

The indwelling Holy Spirit enables a believer to obey God. Review the statements of the men of God quoted above, and take heart.

CHRIST IN US

Christianity is not about trying to live a life like that of Christ or trying to be Christ-like, nor is it Christ giving us the power to live a life like his. Christianity is Christ, by the power of the Holy Spirit, dwelling in Christians and living his life through them.

> *When Christ, who is our life, shall appear, then shall ye also appear with him in glory.*

Colossians 3:4

Christ in us is our hope of glory. His indwelling presence is the only source of true joy.

---

2.   Ibid., (quoting John Bradford, 1555, http://www.thirdmill.org/newfiles/jac_arnold/NT.Arnold.Rom.37.pdf.(accessed, 2006)).

3.   Ibid., (quoting Bishop George Berkley, http://www.thirdmill.org/newfiles/jac_arnold/NT.Arnold.Rom.37.pdf. (accessed ___, ___ 2006)).

GETTING TO KNOW JESUS

It is not enough to cling to what we have learned about Jesus in Sunday school, in sermons, or through books. There are many ways to know him. He reveals himself in scripture, in contemplative prayer, and through acts of love to the least of his brethren.

Most individuals know little about a personal god who dwells in them through his holy spirit. They know even less about his purpose for them in this life, which is a basic source of joy.

In the parable of the marriage feast (Matthew 22:2–14), a king saw a man who had no wedding garment. He asked the man how he had gotten in without the appropriate apparel. The man had no explanation, and the king cast him into the outer darkness. This judgment serves as a chilling warning to those who call themselves believers but do not understand what is required of them.

The more we get to know Jesus and experience his love for us, the more joy we will have in our lives.

PERSISTENCE THROUGH TRIALS

I have always been conscientious. For this and for other reasons, I have not been content with whatever state in which I have found myself. It has been difficult to leave my worries on my doorstep and cross over to the sunny side of the street. Everything depends on my choice of focus.

When we experience adversity, we can search for verses of scripture that will give our souls comfort. We can also find refuge in nature, music, and abiding in the truth.

OUR RESPONSIBILITY

In the flesh, the Christian life is impossible. Only Christ loved God and his neighbors to the extent of dying for their sins. Nevertheless, as we focus our minds on Jesus and reject evil, we grow in the grace and knowledge of our lord and savior, Jesus Christ, and become more like him (2 Peter 3:18). As we grow to be more like Christ, our joy increases.

The ultimate joy will come when we see God face to face in heaven. That joy will be eternal, unending, and beyond anything we can imagine here on earth.

31

Options

How are we to live in a country that is losing its preeminence in the world? What can we do while we watch the decline of our American civilization?

We are not doomed to sit back and simply wait for our nation to fall the way Rome and Jericho did so many years ago. We can live lives of peace, tranquility, and hope even in the midst of this downfall.

Here are some of my ideas on how to survive and thrive in these dark days.

ESCHEW RELATIVISM

Relativism is any theory of ethics or knowledge based on the idea that all values and judgments are relative, differing according to circumstances, persons, and cultures. According to the relativist, each individual has his or her personal understanding of truth, and no one has an ultimate truth. Everyone is supposed to be tolerant of all individuals by condoning their lifestyle choices, whatever those choices may be.

We must not condone the lifestyles of the ungodly for the sake of tolerance, nor must we compromise righteousness for unity. When the occasion arises, expose moral relativism. Take a firm stand against subjectivism until truth prevails. Remember that absolute truth is the only genuine foundation.

FIGHT THE EVIL WITHIN

Many view evil as a force outside themselves. Evil also exists within us. If Satan is the enemy and the symbol of evil from without, your ego is the enemy within. It is through our sensual selves that Satan gains access to lure us away from the path of God and to have us commit evil deeds.

The devil's goal is to destroy us and to keep us away from God. Followers of Christ are the devil's sworn enemies, so we experience his attacks more than those who do not follow him. His most common and subtle methods are deception, doubt, and temptation.

In the account of Adam and Eve, we read that God gave Adam and Eve permission to eat from any tree in the garden except the Tree of Knowledge of Good and Evil. He warned them about the penalty of death if they ate the forbidden fruit.

The devil planted doubt in Eve's mind by asking her if God really had said what she thought he had. Ignoring the rules of God and exaggerating his prohibitions, the devil denied the penalty of death for eating the forbidden fruit. He told Eve, "It won't do you any harm. Why not give it a try?" This deception resulted in disobedience, which destroyed Adam and Eve's relationship with God as well as their relationship with each other.

The devil has been using these same tactics on human beings ever since. But there is good news! The Bible says, "He [God] has delivered us from the dominion of darkness and transferred us to the kingdom of his beloved Son" (Colossians 1:13). The devil has no power over us. We have the authority to command the devil to go to hell.

ATTACK THE ENEMY

Direct demonic possession of people and places is another frightening weapon that the devil has at his disposal. The Bible tells of the many afflictions Satan can cause: "And he (Jesus) healed many who were sick with various diseases, and cast out many demons; and He would not permit the demons to speak, because they knew him" (Mark 1:34).

God gives us spiritual armor and weapons to resist these dark forces of evil. "Put on the whole armor of God that you may be able to stand against the wiles of the devil. For we are not contending against flesh and blood, but against the principalities, against the powers, against the world rulers of this present darkness, against the spiritual hosts of wickedness in the heavenly places. Therefore, take the whole armor of God, that you may be able to withstand in the evil day, and having done all, to stand" (Ephesians 6:11–13).

In Ephesians 6:10–18 is the list of the armor of God:

The belt of truth to counter the devil's lies

The breastplate of righteousness to protect our relationship with God

The shield of faith as a defense against the devil's attacks
The helmet of salvation
The sword of the spirit, which is the word of God
We have also prayer and supplication in our arsenal.

When Jesus was tempted by the devil, he replied from the scriptures. The devil will flee from someone who knows and believes the Bible, because the Bible is truth. (See Ephesians 6:14–18.)

SEEK A BALANCED LIFE

Moderation is the key to a life of peace and tranquility. We must strive to find balance in all areas. Here are a couple of examples.

SOLITUDE AND SERVICE

After Jesus spent time ministering to the crowds, he went up on a mountain by himself to pray (Matthew 14:23). If we want to know our father in heaven, we need time in solitary prayer with God each day.

We cannot live a full life by simply sitting by ourselves and praying. We must also minister to the needy world around us, just as Jesus did.

Time alone is also necessary for refreshing our bodies and souls. Then, when we return to the crowd, we will be better able to minister to the needs of others.

I mentioned contemplative prayer in the chapter on truth. I highly recommend that you practice meditation in order to diminish the brain chatter that debilitates us. Henri Nouwen was a Jesuit priest of the same caliber as Thomas Merton, who was also a Jesuit priest. They were prolific writers who helped me to experience inner solitude. It is certain that you will grow in love when you experience silence. Henri J. M. Nouwen offers some wisdom on solitude:

> Letting our aloneness grow into solitude and not into loneliness is a lifelong struggle. It requires conscious choice about whom to be with, what to study, how to pray, and when to ask for counsel. But wise choices will help us to find the solitude where our hearts can grow in love.[1]

---

1. Henri J. M. Nouwen, *Bread for the Journey: Meditation for January 18* (Harper Collins Publishers, 1997).

RECEIVING AND GIVING

In order for our minds to grow, we need to receive the word of God through in-depth study. In the scriptures, we will find the truth we need to live fulfilling lives. This freeing truth will cause our hearts to overflow with love and a desire to give to others. We must not hoard the pearls of wisdom we discover. Our joy, as well as our knowledge, will grow exponentially when we share biblical truths with others.

TURN THE OTHER CHEEK

We have all experienced some form of injustice. What should we do about it? Let us consider Matthew 5:38–42: "You have heard that it was said, 'An eye for an eye and a tooth for a tooth.' But I say to you, do not resist one who is evil. But if any one strikes you on the right cheek, turn to him the other also; and if any one would sue you and take your coat, let him have your cloak as well; and if any one forces you to go one mile, go with him two miles. Give to him who begs from you, and do not refuse him who would borrow from you."

Jesus did not practice or counsel nonresistance. He never was politically correct, and he did not instruct us to endure injustice from any individual or institution. His instruction is to turn the other cheek.

When you turn the other cheek, you are giving the assailant permission to hit you again. You are not responding with violence. Metaphorically speaking, most of us have been slapped on the cheek and did not respond with personal revenge. Turning the other cheek tells the assailant that you refuse to respond in a similar manner. Depending on the magnitude of the event, the victim can resort to seeking retribution through civil authorities. This alternative, cited here from Larry Pierce's *The New John Gill's Exposition of the Entire Bible*, provides a peaceful resolution instead of an escalation of the conflict: "Not but that a man may lawfully defend himself, and endeavour to secure himself from injuries; and may appear to the civil magistrate for redress of grievances; but he is not to make use of private revenge."[2]

---

2.   Larry Pierce, The New John Gill's Exposition of the Entire Bible (Ontario, Canada: Winterbourne)

We do not have the option of violence. Our insistence on integrity and justice will precipitate conflict with custom and authority. On some occasions, this will require deliberate resistance.

We are not to belittle or hold anyone in contempt, not even those who have treated us unjustly. Shame and humiliation are forms of hate that have psychologically destroyed many individuals. Revenge damages the person who takes revenge as well as the object of that revenge.

TRUST GOD FOR TOMORROW

People are always concerned about the future, but none of us can add one cubit to our lifespan by worrying (Matthew 6:27). I offer three options to redirect anxious thoughts:

Spend more time in nature. The contrast between the finite and the infinite will give you a sense of proportion.

Listen to inspiring music. Music has a powerful effect on our emotions.

Help those who are less fortunate than you are. Community service can be a wonderful way to assist others, and you gain something for yourself along the way. Seeing the despair of others firsthand will reduce your anxiety.

SEEK WISDOM

King Solomon wrote, "The fear of the Lord is the beginning of wisdom, and the knowledge of the Holy One is insight" (Proverbs 9:10). There is no wisdom apart from a respect for God. This respect enables a person to understand what justice is, to recognize when courage is required, and to do the right thing in any circumstance.

In Psalm 73, the psalmist called on his entire mental capacity in order to understand the prosperity of the wicked, but to no avail. He searched the depths of his soul to penetrate the darkness that hid the meaning from him. Finally, the psalmist took his questions and concerns to God. By the grace of God, his spiritual eyes were opened and his heart was illuminated as the lord showed him the true state of the wicked.

Wisdom is a divine secret that can only be revealed by God.

PURSUE TRUTH

Pursue truth with earnest, conscientious, unflagging zeal. Speak the truth at all times and in all places. Live in the truth, and you will have a pure heart. We need pure hearts to experience God's goodness.

Truth must be the first test of all that you think, say, and do. If words are not true, do not speak them. If a behavior is not true, do not practice it. If a thought is not true, discard it from your mind as quickly as possible. The world needs honest people in all occupations.

Let truth pursue you. Let truth grasp you. Let truth know you. Ultimately, let truth master you.

Always challenge a liar, regardless of his relationship to you or his status in the community. Present the truth to him with love.

God is truth, and we should worship him. Individuals who have a personal relationship with Christ should always be making their way toward the truth. God will progressively reveal truth to those who worship and seek him with all their hearts.

BE AMBITIOUS FOR GOD

Shakespeare missed the mark when he spoke through Cardinal Wolsey and told Cromwell to flee ambition.[3] He suggested that ambition is destructive. At times, it might be; however, when properly utilized, ambition can enable men to do great things. Eschew ambitions for fame, power, and wealth; instead, ambitiously feed God's sheep.

OUR RESPONSIBILITY

The only way to live a life of peace and harmony, hope and joy in the dark days ahead is to accept the salvation God has provided, to meditate on him and his word daily, and to live a godly life of righteousness in spite of the rampant unrighteousness all around us.

---

3.   Shakespeare's Henry VIII. Act III, scene 2 (c.f., http://www. shakespeare-literature.com/)

32

Farewell

As I considered how to end this book, I felt Satan urging me to skip the subject of death. In spite of this temptation, I have chosen to speak the truth and write about death.

Throughout this book, we have been addressing the death of America culture, our survival of this death, and the death of the will. Death is a fundamental part of the search for truth.

DEATH AND JUDGMENT

When mortals die, their spirits will be eternally with God in heaven or eternally with the devil in hell. In Hebrews 9: 27, it is recorded: "In as much as it is appointed for men to die once, then comes the judgment."

> In Matthews 7: 21–23 it is recorded: "Not every one who says to me, 'Lord, Lord,' shall enter the kingdom of heaven, but he who does the will of my Father who is in heaven. On that day, many will say to me, 'Lord, Lord, did we not prophesy in your name, and cast out demons in your name, and do many mighty works in your name?' And then will I declare to them, 'I never knew you; depart from me, you evildoers.'"

God will give great rewards to those who are diligently serving him. On the other hand, the wrath of God will come down from heaven against all ungodly and wicked men who suppress the truth (Romans 1:18). "The times of ignorance God overlooked, but now he commands all men everywhere to repent, because he has fixed a day on which he will judge the world in righteousness by a man whom he has appointed, and of this, He has given assurance to all men by raising him from the dead" (Acts 17:30–31).

God is absolute love, but he is also just. He must judge sin, even though he wants all people to be with him in heaven. Jesus Christ solved that dilemma. If you believe and ask Jesus to come into your heart, he will.

FOUR TYPES OF PEOPLE

In Matthew 13:18–23, Jesus tells a parable about four kinds of people:

> When any one hears the word of the kingdom and does not understand it, the evil one comes and snatches away what is sown in his heart; this is what was sown along the path.
>
> As for what was sown on rocky ground, this is he who hears the word and immediately receives it with joy; yet he has no root in himself, but endures for a while, and when tribulation or persecution arises because of the word, immediately he falls away.
>
> As for what was sown among thorns, this is he who hears the word, but the cares of the world and the delight in riches choke the word, and it proves unfruitful.
>
> As for what was sown on good soil, this is he who hears the word and understands it; he indeed bears fruit, and yields, in one case a hundredfold, in another sixty, and in another thirty.

The four types of soil represent the hearts of individuals, each responding differently to the gospel. Christ sows the word of God. The first listener hears but does not understand; consequently, Satan snatches the word from him. The second listener is excited about the gospel but lacks the endurance to follow Christ; he does not consider the cost of discipleship. The third listener focuses on the things of this world, not on Christ. About this fellow, Jesus said, "For what does it profit a man, to gain the whole world and forfeit his life?" (Mark 8:36). The receptive listener acts on his understanding of the word.

THE LIVES OF THE SAINTS

My spiritual life has been deeply affected by reading about the lives of St. John of the Cross, St. Therese of Avila, St. Anthony, St. Francis of Assisi, St. Augustine, and St. Thomas Aquinas. All of these saints were human beings who struggled and persevered in their battle against their fallen human nature. They experienced every imaginable type of situation. Reading their life stories helps motivate me to persevere in my own battles.

Our adversaries are the world, the flesh, and the devil. Of the three, our own fallen human nature is the most powerful. Most of our trouble does not come from the devil as much as from our fallen human nature.

St. Thomas Aquinas's sister asked him what she needed to do to become a saint. He answered in two words: "Will it."[1] If we truly want something, we will do all that is necessary to attain it.

St. Augustine prayed, "Lord, let me know myself in order that I may know Thee."[2] If we truly want to know and love Jesus, we must realize what a fallen human nature we have and the struggles that we must overcome.

Let us follow the examples of the saints: pray for the grace to be true to ourselves, strive to overcome our faults, and daily die to ourselves.

WE ARE ALL SAINTS

In all my studies, it never occurred to me to ask what I must do to become a saint. As I was writing this chapter, I decided to find out. Again, I felt Satan urging me not to find out how to be more holy, and urging me to stop telling others about Jesus. In spite of this temptation, I chose to speak the truth and write about saints.

Webster's New World College Dictionary has this definition for "saint": "In certain Christian churches, a person officially recognized as having lived an exceptionally holy life, and thus as being in heaven and capable of interceding for sinners."

Our Lord says to all of us, "You, therefore, must be perfect, as your heavenly Father is perfect" (Matthew 5:48). And: "If you love me, you will keep my commandments" (John 14:15).

Open your mind and heart to God's grace, obey the law of God, and cooperate with his grace.

---

1.   Rev. Fr. Benedict Hughes, "Lord, That I May Know Myself…" (CMRI), as quoted in http://www.cmri.org/01-fmb-self.html. (accessed January 10, 2007)

2.   Ibid.

OUR PREDOMINANT FAULTS

We all have a predominant fault in our spiritual life. We must pray for the grace to see it. When we discover our predominant fault, we must examine our conscience daily and work at eradicating this sin.

By the grace of God and our efforts, we can overcome every temptation. We are free to sin or to eschew sinning. If something is impossible to overcome, it cannot be a sin.

Some people do not try to overcome their predominant fault, thus they reduce their freedom.

CROSSROAD

We now come to a crossroad. A crossroad is one road crossing over another. We cannot be on both roads at the same time. Adam and Eve encountered a crossroad in the beginning of time: "The serpent said to the woman, 'You will not die. For God knows that when you eat of it your eyes will be opened, and you will be like God, knowing good and evil'" (Genesis 3:4–5).

Satan lied. We all will die. We cannot open our eyes without the Holy Spirit. We will never be like God.

The truth is that whoever believes that Jesus Christ, God's only son, died for their transgressions will inherit life everlasting. God resurrected Christ from the dead, and he will do likewise for all believers.

God created us to follow Jesus Christ (to be the image of God in this world) and to make disciples for him and thus spread his kingdom throughout all the nations of the world. When we do this, we reflect the glory of God to the world around us.

THE WRONG ROAD

The road that leads to destruction is easy and the gate is wide; therefore, many people are lured to it. (See Matthew 7:13.) "Their feet run to evil, and they rush to shed innocent blood; their thoughts are thoughts of iniquity, desolation and destruction are in their highways. The way of peace they do not know, and there is no justice in their paths. Their roads they have made crooked; no one who walks in them knows peace" (Isaiah 59:7–8).

Although many want paradise, those who refuse to be faithful by serving Christ will not be able to enter. (See Matthew 7:13–14 and Luke 13:23–24.) Jesus admonished his followers, "Be faithful until death, and I will give you the crown of life" (Revelation 2:10).

THE RIGHT ROAD

Man thinks he knows the right way, but in the end, it leads to death. (See Proverbs 14:12.) He does not have the spiritual discernment to choose the right road. (See Jeremiah 10:23.) So God provided the way for his people. Only the pure in heart shall travel on it. (See Isaiah 35:8.)

Jesus said, "The one who believes and is baptized will be saved; but the one who does not believe will be condemned" (Mark 16:16).

Paul wrote, "So faith comes from what is heard, and what is heard comes through the word of Christ" (Romans 10:17).

WHICH ROAD ARE YOU ON?

You know that you are on the right road if it leads you to the right destination. You are on the wrong road if it takes you to the wrong destination. Are you traveling on the right road now?

OUR RESPONSIBILITY

Christ is the only way to survive the fall of the American empire, or even to survive this earthly life. If you have not done so already, I urge you to make a commitment to Jesus Christ right here and now. Although you and I have never met face to face, I sincerely hope you will pursue the truth and seek the kingdom of God and his righteousness.

In parting, let me share with you our lord's words of farewell to his disciples, which he spoke to them just before he ascended to heaven:

> I will pray to the Father, and he will give you another Counselor, to be with you forever, even the Spirit of truth, whom the world cannot receive, because it neither sees him nor knows him; you know him, for he dwells with you, and will be in you.

I will not leave you desolate; I will come to you. Yet a little while, and the world will see me no more, but you will see me; because I live, you will live also. In that day, you will know that I am in my Father, and you in me, and I in you. He who has my commandments and keeps them, he it is who loves me; and he who loves me will be loved by my Father, and I will love him and manifest myself to him.
(John 14:16–21)